Music Express

Year 3

LESSON PLANS, RECORDINGS, ACTIVITIES, PHOTOCOPIABLES AND VIDEOCLIPS

Compiled by Maureen Hanke   Illustrated by Alison Dexter   Edited by Emily Haward

A & C Black • London

Contents

First published 2002
Reprinted 2002, 2003, 2004
by A & C Black Publishers Ltd
37, Soho Square, London W1D 3QZ
© 2002 A & C Black Publishers Ltd

Teaching text © Maureen Hanke 2002
Unit headings, unit summary text, learning objectives and
outcomes © Qualifications and Curriculum Authority
CD/Videoclips compilation © A & C Black 2002
Edited by Emily Haward
Designed by Jocelyn Lucas
Cover illustration © Alex Ayliffe 2002
Inside illustrations © Alison Dexter 2002
Audio CD sound engineering by Stephen Chadwick
Videoclips filmed and edited by Jamie Acton-Bond
CD-ROM post production by Ian Shepherd
at Sound Recording Technology

Printed in Great Britain by Caligraving Ltd, Thetford, Norfolk

A & C Black uses paper produced with elemental chlorine-free
pulp, harvested from managed sustainable forests.

Introduction

About Music Express

Music Express provides teaching activities that are imaginative, inspiring and fun.

It has been written especially for classroom teachers. It is:

- user-friendly;
- well planned;
- fully resourced, and
- no music reading is required.

Using Music Express as a scheme of work

National Curriculum

Music Express fulfils the requirements of the Music National Curriculum of England, of Wales and of Northern Ireland and the 5-14 National Guidelines for Scotland.

Learning with *Music Express*, children will gain a broad and balanced musical education. They will:

- learn about and sing songs from around the world including the British Isles;
- learn about music from different periods and genres;
- enjoy music lessons with a balance of listening, composing, performing and appraising.

A steady progression plan has been built into *Music Express*, both within each book and from one year to the next, ensuring consistent musical development.

Opportunities are identified throughout for evaluating the children's work and monitoring their progress.

The English QCA scheme of work for music

Music Express is based on the structure of the QCA scheme of work. It uses the same unit headings, and provides activities for all the learning objectives and outcomes.

The teaching activities in *Music Express* have been drawn from and inspired by A & C Black's extensive classroom music resources.

The units

There are six units in each book. Below is a list of the units in *Music Express Year 3*, as described by the QCA:

Animal magic
'This unit develops children's ability to create, perform and analyse short descriptive compositions that combine sounds, movements and words.'

Play it again
'This unit develops children's ability to create simple rhythmic patterns and perform them rhythmically using notation as a support.'

The class orchestra
'This unit develops children's ability to create, combine and perform rhythmic and melodic material as part of a class performance of a song.'

Dragon scales
'This unit develops children's ability to recognise, and use, pentatonic scales and create short melodies and accompaniments.'

Painting with sound
'This unit develops children's ability to create, perform and analyse expressive compositions and extend their sound vocabulary.'

Salt pepper vinegar mustard
'This unit develops children's ability to recognise and explore some characteristics of singing games. It consolidates their sense of pulse and ability to perform with others.'

The lessons

Each unit is divided into six, weekly lessons, which are intended to be taught over a half term.

There are three activities per lesson which may be taught in one longer music lesson, or over three shorter lessons to suit your timetable.

Planning

The CD-ROM

The CD-ROM provides a medium term plan and six, weekly lesson plans for each unit. These may be printed out to go in your planning folder.

Whilst it is not necessary when teaching the activities to have the lesson plan alongside, it contains useful information for preparing your lesson. This includes:

- the learning objectives and outcomes;

- a list of the resources and minimal preparation you will need to do before the lesson;

- a vocabulary section which defines the musical terms appropriate to the lesson;

- a suggestion of ways to provide differentiated support for particular activities;

- a lesson extension - a suggestion for taking the lesson further with individuals or the whole class. (The extension activities are particularly useful when teaching a mixed year-group class as they extend the older and/or more able children.)

The book

The book provides step by step teaching notes for each lesson. These are written to be as easy to follow as possible.

There are photocopiables to supplement many of the activities.

Preparation

Music Express is designed to minimise your preparation time.

Look out for the icons next to the activity headings which indicate things you need to prepare.

Key to icons

Photocopiable icon: some activities require photocopies or activity cards to be made from a particular photocopiable.

CD icon: you will need to have access to a CD player for an activity.

Videoclip and picture icons: you will need to have access to a computer for an activity to show videoclips and pictures on the CD-ROM. (You might like to use a computer-compatible projector to show the videoclips and pictures on a screen for the whole class to see more easily.)

Other resources

Classroom percussion

You will need to have a range of classroom percussion instruments available.

Many activities suggest several members of the class playing instruments at the same time. If necessary, pupils could share instruments and take turns to play.

Specific activities recommend the instruments you will need, but you should use the instruments that you have available.

For a class of 30 pupils, aim to have at least the following:

- Tuned percussion
    - 1 alto xylophone
    - 1 alto metallophone
    - 1 set of chime bars
    - a selection of beaters
- A range of untuned percussion instruments, eg
    - tambours
    - drums
    - wood blocks
    - cabassas
    - maracas

- Other interesting soundmakers, eg
    - ocean drum
    - rainmaker
    - whistles
    - wind chimes
    - Electronic keyboards are a very useful resource and should be included wherever possible.

Instrumental lessons

Wherever appropriate, invite members of the class who are having instrumental lessons to bring their instruments into classroom music lessons.

If you are not sure which notes particular instruments use, ask the child's instrumental teacher.

Recording and evaluating

Recording on cassette or video

Have a cassette recorder and blank audio cassettes available during your music lessons. Recording pupils' work is important for monitoring their progress.

Children enjoy listening to their performances and contributing to the evaluation of their own and their classmates' work.

Many activities include movement as well as music. If you have a video camera available, video the performance. If not, invite members of your class or another class to watch and offer feedback.

Help for teachers

Teaching tips and background information

These are provided throughout next to the activity or activities to which they refer.

Dance and movement

Encourage movement in activities where it is not mentioned - it is an important means of musical learning.

Group work

The activities suggest appropriate group sizes. Be flexible, especially if your class has little or no experience of group work. Group work may be introduced into classroom music lessons gradually. Those activities which suggest group work may also be managed as whole class activities.

Teaching songs

We hope that teachers will lead the singing with their own voice, particularly with younger children. But in all instances we have assumed that the teacher will use the CD.

If you feel confident, teach yourself a song using the CD and then teach it to the children.

To rehearse songs with your class without the CD, you might:
- sing the melody without the words, to lah or dee;
- chant the rhythm of the words;
- sing the song line by line for the children to copy.

Teachers' videoclips

There are seventeen videoclips on the CD-ROM that demonstrate useful teaching techniques to use in class music lessons.

Clip	Contents
T 01	The Music Express Song
T 02	Teaching a song line by line
T 03	Demonstrating pitch with hand
T 04	Starting together: speed and starting note
T 05	Internalising
T 06	Conducting with a score
T 07	Conducting getting louder
T 08	Inventing vocal ostinatos
T 09	Dividing a class into groups
T 10	Conducting start and stop
T 11	Building layers of sound
T 12	Playing a drone accompaniment
T 13	Recognising a word rhythm
T 14	Allocating accompaniment instruments
T 15	Conducting instrumental groups
T 16	Helping to perform a steady beat
T 17	Putting instruments away

Ongoing skills

'Ongoing skills' are identified by the QCA scheme of work as those skills which need to be continually developed and revisited. This is in addition to the activities in the six units. The QCA suggests that learning may take place as the opportunity arises throughout the school week, eg in short 5-minute sessions.

Music Express does not include a separate Ongoing skills unit, but addresses the skills throughout its activities. When using *Music Express* as a scheme, you will be fulfilling the learning objectives and outcomes of the QCA Ongoing skills unit.

If you teach music in one weekly lesson, as opposed to three shorter lessons, you may like to select activities from *Music Express* for supplementary 5-minute activities. By doing this, you will reinforce more regularly the development of the musical skills identified by the QCA.

Extension and future learning

A & C Black website

Music Express provides all the resources you will need for teaching a year of music. We hope, however, that you will use other songs and activities to ring the changes in subsequent years or to link with other National Curriculum subjects.

The website www.acblack.com/musicexpress lists the *Music Express* activities that were drawn from or inspired by other A & C Black books, and links to other books that will supplement the activities in *Music Express*.

TORTOISE SONG

1 Discuss how different animals are described by the words and music in *Tortoise song*

- Listen to *Tortoise song*, then ask the children these questions:
  - what words are used to describe each animal? *(eg orang-utans are big and hairy.)*
  - according to the words, which animal is the slowest? *(The tortoise.)*
  - how does the music reinforce this? *(The notes of the melody are longer and smoother than those for the other animals. Only a few notes are used and they are close together; no jumps. You can imagine a tortoise moving with very slow, smooth movements.)*

Teaching tip
- You may want to listen to the song a few times to find out the answers to these questions.

- All sing *Tortoise song*. In the chorus, demonstrate the shape of the tortoise tune by moving your hand a little higher and lower as the pitch of the melody goes higher and lower.

V1 Orang-utans are big and hairy,
　 Kangaroos are always on the go,
　 Polar bears are kind of scary,
　 Give me something sensible and slow.

Ch A tortoise takes its time,
　 It tends to travel in a slow, straight line.
　 A tortoise takes its time,
　 A friend of a tortoise is a friend of mine.

V2 Porcupines are plump and prickly,
　 Roadrunners are raring for a race,
　 Quails are quaint at moving quickly,
　 I prefer a smooth and steady pace.

Repeat the chorus

2 Prepare movements to add to the song

- Listen to track 2 to become familiar with the length of gap between each line of the verses. Decide how animals might greet each other with actions in these gaps in the song, eg
  - kangaroos gently box in the air with their front feet

box　　　box

1	2	1	2	1	+	2	+	1	+	2	+
Kan-ga-roos		are al - ways on		the go,							
					(box,	box,	box,	box,	box,	box,	box)

  - porcupines display their prickles *(spread fingers wide in the air)*

pri　-　ckle

1	2	1	2	1	+	2	+	1	+	2	+
Por - cu-pines		are plump and prick	-	ly,							
					(pri - ckle,		pri - ckle,		pri - ckle)		

- Practise each greeting in time with the CD.

3 Perform *Tortoise song* with mimed greetings and tuned percussion accompaniment

- Small groups practise the tortoise tune on tuned percussion using the photocopiable and track 3.

- All perform *Tortoise song* with track 1. A small group plays the tortoise tune and everyone else sings and mimes the greetings as practised. *(The first time the song is sung, the tortoise tune is played in the choruses only. When the song repeats, it continues throughout.)*

Tortoise tune

ANIMALS IN MUSIC

1 **Discuss the use of words and music in *Sea slugs and jellyfish* and in *Seagulls***

- Listen to *Sea slugs and jellyfish* (track 4), then ask this question:

  – how are sea slugs and jellyfish described by the words and music?
  (Sea slugs are huge, slow, fat, and blow bubbles. The melody uses long, low notes. Jellyfish are slimy, mauve, bloated and transparent. They quiver, shiver and float. When the jellyfish quivers, the melody quivers by alternating between two notes. When the jellyfish floats, the melody floats on long, held notes.)

- Listen to *Seagulls* (track 5), then discuss these questions:

  – how effective is the music in describing seagulls?
  (There are good sound effects for mimicking the call of a seagull. The mood of the music is gentle. It is easy to imagine seagulls flying around.)

  – what might the raspberry sound represent?
  (Listen to suggestions and then play the sung version of Seagulls (track 6) to find out the humorous answer.)

Teaching tips

- You might need to play *Sea slugs and jellyfish* several times to find out the answer to this question.

- Encourage the children to move their hands like a bird whilst they listen to *Seagulls*. Notice how the mood of the music influences how they move their hands.

- The sound effect for the call of the seagull is made by blowing the top section of a recorder very gently.

2 **Listen to one composer's descriptions of different animals in music**

- *Tortoises* (track 7) - Tell the children the title, then listen to the music. Ask how the music describes tortoises.
  (The music is slow, as tortoises traditionally are. The melody uses long, smooth notes that never travel very far. It is a very slow version of the music used for the Can-can.)

- *Kangaroos* (track 8) - Tell the children the title, then listen to the music. Ask how the music describes kangaroos.
  (The piano is played as if a kangaroo is jumping up the piano keyboard, landing on clusters of notes from the low notes of the piano to the high notes.)

- Can the class guess this animal (track 9) by listening for clues in the music?
  (Elephant. The clues are: the music uses low-pitched notes, has a strong, steady beat and is slightly lumbering in places.)

3 **Move in character to the music of *Bear dance***

- Listen to *Bear dance*.

- Explain that the music is about a bear. Ask what sort of character the children think this bear is.
  (The music suggests a large, friendly bear that moves steadily and heavily with a strong steady beat, and possibly a little awkwardly.)

- Mime walking as a bear in time with the music.

Background information

- *Tortoises*, *Kangaroos* and *The elephant* are extracts from *The Carnival of the animals* written by the French composer Saint-Saëns in 1886.

- The work is a grand zoological fantasy in fourteen movements, each representing a different animal. The children may enjoy listening to some of the other movements if you have a recording.

ANIMAL HASTHAS

1 **Watch some traditional Indian dance movements for different animals**

- Explain that traditional Indian dance has specific movements for certain animals.

- All watch videoclips 1-7 closely and afterwards discuss how each animal is represented.
(*The hands make the shape of a small animal or a characteristic part of a large animal, eg the two elephant gestures are for the trunk and ear. The hands are moved in a way that represents how the animal moves, so the bird gently flits around in the air, and the snake slithers around. For some animals, such as the deer, the dancer uses full body movements rather than just hands.*)

Teaching tip

- If you have a computer-compatible projector, you could show the class these videoclips on a large screen.

2 **Learn the hand movements for different animals**

- Use the photocopiable to learn the Indian hand shapes for the animals on the videoclips.

- Practise the movements, encouraging the children to let their hands take on the personality and mood of the different animals.

- Watch the videoclips again to improve technique.

3 **Improvise hand movements to accompany the music, *Raga abhogi***

- Listen to *Raga abhogi* (tracks 11-12) and ask the children to think about which of the animals studied in activity 2 they can most easily imagine moving in time to this music. Explain that this music is not about a particular animal, so their decision is entirely their own choice.

- Play the track again. The children improvise moving their hands as their chosen animal in time with the music.

- Ask individuals to share what they were imagining as they did their improvisations. Did they act out a story? What did they think happened to their animal when the speed of the music changed (*track 12*)?

- Watch a videoclip showing an improvisation to the same music (*videoclip 8*). Encourage the children to notice how the dancer watches her hand movements with her eyes and uses facial expressions as well as movement to describe what she feels is happening.

- The children move to the music again. Encourage them to be more imaginative with their movements.

Teaching tips

- Watch to see how the class responds to the change in the speed of the music.

- Make a note of the children who notice the change of speed immediately and adapt their movements in an obvious way.

Hand shapes

tortoise
kurma hastha

bee
bhramara hastha

deer 3
simhamukha hastha

snake 4
sarpasirsa hastha

tiger 5
viyakraha hastha

bird 6
garuda hastha

elephant 7
mukula hastha

elephant 7
hamsasya hastha

SOUNDS LIKE AN ANIMAL MOVING!

1 Think of words to describe animal movements 🔊13-14))

- Listen to track 13. Explain that this is one way music might represent an animal walking. *(It is a simple steady beat.)*

- As a class, make a list of words that describe other ways animals move, eg jumping, flying ... Encourage individuals to demonstrate their suggestions.

- Listen to track 14. Ask what movement is being represented this time, and why. Again, encourage individuals to demonstrate their suggestion with body movements in time to the music.
(Flying, gliding, swooping or swimming are all possible answers, because they might all be reflected by this gentle up and down movement on the xylophone.)

Teaching tip

- Encourage the children to think specifically of the movements linked to animals from previous weeks: orang-utans, kangaroos, polar bears, tortoises, porcupines, roadrunners, quails, sea slugs, jellyfish, seagulls, elephants, bears, bees, deer, snakes and tigers.

2 Invent music to represent animal movements

- Invite a volunteer to demonstrate an animal 'jumping' using tuned percussion, eg

- Can anyone demonstrate the animal jumping higher? *(eg play from a lower note to a higher one.)*
- Can anyone demonstrate the animal jumping faster? *(eg play the notes faster.)*
- Invite another volunteer to demonstrate an animal 'running' using untuned percussion, eg

- Can anyone demonstrate the animal running faster? *(eg tapping the drum faster.)*
- Can anyone demonstrate the animal slowing down to a walk? *(eg the tapping might slow down to a walking pace.)*
- Invite a volunteer to demonstrate the difference between an old animal running and a young animal running. *(eg the old animal runs at a slower pace.)*

3 Extend the animal movements into a sequence 🔊15-16))

- Listen to two examples of sequences:
    - track 15 - a bird takes off, flies, then lands;
    - track 16 - an animal walks, then runs, then jumps.

- Ask pairs to invent a sequence of three animal movements using only two classroom percussion instruments *(as in the examples on the CD)*. Encourage each pair to make the join from one movement to another as smooth as possible so that the three ideas blend into one invention.

- Each pair practises their sequence then performs it to the class.

Teaching tips

- Encourage as many children as possible to have a go at demonstrating their ideas.
- Encourage the children to try their ideas on different instruments.

A MOVING STORY

1 Write a description of an animal's movements

- All sing *Tortoise song*.
- Pairs of children choose one of the animals from the song and talk about movements it makes. These may be real or imaginary, eg eating, hunting, moving, cleaning its teeth ...
- Each pair writes a narration about their chosen animal. It might be:
  - a description of its daily routine
  - a description of a special event, eg its birthday, a day out...
  - its appearance on a TV animal documentary
- When the narrations are complete, share them with the class.

> **Teaching tip**
> - Explain that they will be adding movement then music to their narration, so they should take that into consideration when choosing their animal.

2 Add movement to the animal narrations

- Pairs create a mime of their animal narration. They may include the hastha movements they have already learnt if they wish. If necessary, they may decide to refine their narrations to be more effective with the mime.
- When they have developed their ideas, one child narrates while the other performs the mime. They should practise synchronising the words and movements.

3 Perform the animal narrations and mimes

- Each pair performs to the class.
- As a class, discuss which performances were the most effective (*eg dramatically spoken narration, good timing between narrator and actor, fantastically exaggerated movements*).
- Ask what made some performances better than others and encourage suggestions for improvement, eg
  - speak slower and more clearly with a louder voice
  - include some humour
  - impersonate a television personality
  - move with more exaggeration
  - use full body movements and facial expressions

ANIMAL MINIATURES

1 Develop an animal narration and mime as a group

- Two pairs join together and choose one of their narrations to work on. Encourage the groups to consider which narration might better lend itself to a musical accompaniment.

- Explain that each group is going to perform an *Animal miniature* which includes music, narration and mime. Each group decides who will perform each role.

- Each group chooses two instruments for their miniature. They should consider:

    – how big the animal is *(a large animal could be represented by low notes and a small animal by high notes)*;

    – whether the animal makes any long, continuous movements *(they would need an instrument that can make a continuous sound, eg shaking a tambourine)*;

    – whether the animal makes any short, sudden movements *(they would need an instrument that can play short notes, eg tapping a woodblock)*.

Teaching tips

As you help each group work on the musical part of the performance, encourage them to think about:

- the general speed the animal moves *(tempo)*;

- how loudly the animal moves *(dynamics)*;

- whether the animal moves in a regular pattern or unevenly *(rhythm)*.

2 Add music to the narration and mime

- Each group develops the music for their *Animal miniature* and includes it with the narration and mime.

- Each group practises performing their *Animal miniature.* Encourage them to think about how to start and finish their performance *(eg start and finish in silence, and decide who will give the cue to begin and to finish)*.

- Invite groups to demonstrate their work in progress and ask the class to give feedback for improvement.

3 Perform and evaluate the final *Animal miniatures*

- Each group has a final practice of their *Animal miniatures.*

- Each group performs to the class. If you have a video camera in school, video the performances. Alternatively, invite another class to be an audience.

- Evaluate how successful each group's performance was. Invite members of the class to suggest the two best features of each performance.

1st
Play it again
Exploring rhythmic patterns

RHYTHM GAMES

1 Play *Switch I* and *Switch II* using body percussion

- Stand in a circle to play *Switch I* (*the three examples below are demonstrated on videoclip 9*). The leader claps a simple rhythm pattern that lasts four beats, eg

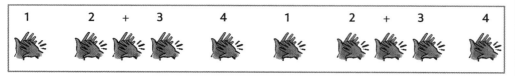

1	2	+	3	4	1	2	+	3	4

- Everyone joins in and when they have settled into the pattern, the leader calls SWITCH and changes their pattern. The class joins in with the new pattern. Use a variety of body percussion patterns, eg

1	2	3	4	1	2	3	4

- Invite individuals to lead the game. Suggest they think of words to fit their pattern to help them remember, eg

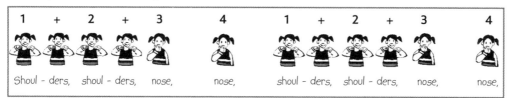

1	+	2	+	3	4	1	+	2	+	3	4
Shoul - ders,		shoul - ders,		nose,	nose,	shoul - ders,		shoul - ders,		nose,	nose,

- *Switch II* starts in the same way, but once the first rhythm is settled the leader changes their pattern whilst the rest of the class continue the existing pattern. Once the leader is confident that the class are familiar with the new pattern they call SWITCH and the class changes immediately to the new pattern (*see videoclip 10*).

Teaching tips

- The children may find it helpful if you count them in at the start of the game: 1 2 3 4.
- It may be helpful also to mouth the beat (1 2 3 4) for them throughout so that they can start each new pattern on beat 1.
- While you learn the game it is better for you, the teacher, to be the leader.

Background information

- *Polka* was composed by Alexander Borodin (1833-87).
- He wrote this piano duet for himself and his adopted daughter, Liza, to play together.

2 Play *Switch II* using untuned percussion instruments

- Play *Switch II* again, as described above, but this time as many children as possible use untuned percussion instruments, the rest clap. Take it in turns to use the percussion instruments.
(*For examples of playing Switch II with instruments, see videoclip 11.*)

3 Listen to the repeated pattern in *Polka*

- Listen to *Polka* (*track 17*), and notice the continuously repeating pattern (*known as Chopsticks*). Listen to track 18 to hear a demonstration of this pattern on its own.

- All play the repeating pattern in the air on an imaginary piano in time with the piano on the recording (*track 17*). Use the index finger of each hand - your hands should get wider apart with the music.

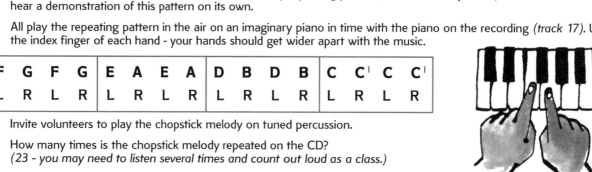

F	G	F	G	E	A	E	A	D	B	D	B	C	C'	C	C'
L	R	L	R	L	R	L	R	L	R	L	R	L	R	L	R

- Invite volunteers to play the chopstick melody on tuned percussion.

- How many times is the chopstick melody repeated on the CD?
(*23 - you may need to listen several times and count out loud as a class.*)

- Explain that a repeated pattern in music is called an 'ostinato' and is used widely in music.

MR NOAH RAP

1 Listen to the rap *Please, Mr Noah*

- Listen to the rap then discuss the story. Ask the children why Noah got more than he bargained for. *(It became very noisy.)*

- Listen again. All join in clicking or tapping the steady beat throughout.

- Listen again to each animal entering the ark and all follow each animal's sound on the *Rapping rhythms* photocopiable.
(Notice how long each sound lasts, eg the snake's hissing sound lasts for four beats, the crocodile says snip snap snip snap on each of the four beats.)

- Ask what happens when all the animals are inside the ark.
(Each animal makes its noise and continues to do so until they are all making their noises at the same time.)

Teaching tips

In this activity, each group needs to be able to perform their rhythm and action to the same steady beat.

- When rehearsing each group, count and tap four steady beats to bring all the children in together.

- At intervals, play the recording to remind everyone of the beat.

- When the groups combine their rhythms, lead the class by counting or tapping a steady beat all the time –
1,2,3,4,1,2,3,4

- They might need to practise several times combining all six groups.

2 Learn the rhythm patterns for each animal

- Divide into six groups, one for each of the animals mentioned in the rap *(snakes, crocodiles, rabbits, lions, monkeys, elephants)*. Each group learns its rhythm pattern using the photocopiable.

- Once they are confident with the rhythm, each group adds an action, either their own invention or the one suggested on the photocopiable:

  – snake: move arm like a snake

  – crocodile: move arms like a crocodile's mouth

  – rabbit: hop, hop, jump on the spot

  – lion: put hands to your mouth as you roar

  – monkey: close and open hands

  – elephant: stamp your foot

- Each group performs their rhythm and action to the class in time to a steady beat.

- Keeping the same steady beat, build up a class performance. The first group starts their rhythm and action and then keeps on repeating it followed by the other groups joining in in turn. Agree a hand signal in advance for 'stop', and either stop each group in turn or all at the same time.

3 Perform the *Please, Mr Noah* rap with the rhythm patterns

- The children practise adding their action and rhythm pattern with the performance on CD track 19.

- When they are certain about where their action and rhythm pattern fit in, practise performing to track 20 - this leaves gaps where the rhythm patterns occur. Each group practises fitting their rhythm pattern and action in the correct gaps and then building cumulatively once inside the ark *(as practised in activity 2)* until Noah says STOP! *(Listen to track 19 whenever necessary to help the groups add their rhythm patterns at the correct time.)*

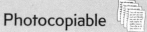
Rapping rhythms

1	+	2	+	3	+	4	+
o							
ssssssssssssssssssssssssssssssssssssssssssssssssssssssssssssssssssssssssssssss							
snip		snap		snip		snap	
hop	and	stop		hop	and	stop	
roarrrrrrrrrrrrrrrrrrrrrrrrrrrrrrrrrrrrr				roarrrrrrrrrrrrrrrrrrrrrrrrrrrrrrrrrrr			
chit –	ter	chat –	ter	chit –	ter	chat –	ter
stomp		a	–	longgggggggggggggggggggggggggggg			

SPACE SHUTTLE RAP

1 Create a Space shuttle rap

- Ask the children to imagine that Noah is building a space shuttle today to take gifts from our planet to another. The gifts may be things that we believe represent our world or our favourite objects *(eg wheelchairs, Playstations™, fresh air ...)*.

- Listen to *Space shuttle rap (track 21)*, then make a list of six different objects that the class would like Noah to take in the shuttle. Make them fit the rap, eg:

Please Mr Noah,
We love the world we inhabit,
Will you take these gifts
To another planet?

I've gotta say yes,
I can't say no,
Just make your sound and
In you go.

Where are the wheelchairs?

— — — — — — — — — — — —

Well done wheelchairs, and
In you go!

Where are the Playstations™?

— — — — — — — — — — — —

Well done Playstations™, and
In you go!

2 Invent and practise the rhythm patterns of chosen objects

- Divide into six groups, one for each of the items chosen in activity 1. Each group invents a rhythm pattern for their item *(this might be a spoken rhythm or vocal sound)*, eg *(track 22)*:

Where are the wheelchairs?
Whirrrrrrrrr, whirrrrrrrrr ...

Where are the Playstations™?
Beep beep beep beep shhhhhhhhh ...

- Each group invents an action to go with the rhythm pattern, eg

  – wheelchairs: move one hand round in a circle

  – Playstations™: with your thumbs, press an imaginary keypad for the 'beeps';

  bang knuckles together as an explosion for the 'shhhhhhhhh'.

- Each group performs their rhythm pattern and action to the class in time to a steady beat.

Teaching tips

- When rehearsing each group, count and tap four steady beats to bring all the children in together.

- When each group performs their rhythm, lead the class by counting or tapping a steady beat all the time – 1,2,3,4, 1,2,3,4

- Invite a confident child to play a steady beat of four counts throughout.

3 Perform the Space shuttle rap to the backing track

- Decide an order for the items to go into the shuttle.

- Perform the *Space shuttle rap* to the backing track. All join in with the rap. Each group performs their rhythm and action at the appropriate time. *(You might like to invite a volunteer to rap the part of Noah throughout.)*

Teaching tips

- After performing the Space shuttle rap for the first time, discuss with the class how the performance went.

- Perform a second time, aiming to improve the performance.

Space shuttle gifts

Please, Mr Noah,
We love the world we inhabit,
Will you take these gifts
To another planet?

I've gotta say yes,
I can't say no,
Just make your sound and
In you go!

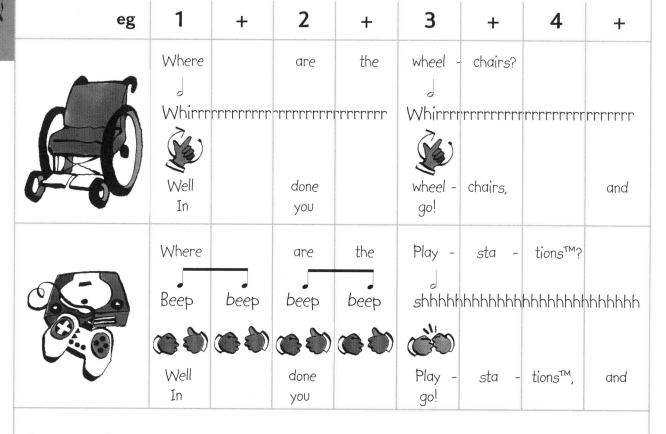

eg	1	+	2	+	3	+	4	+
	Where		are	the	wheel -	chairs?		
	Whirrrrrrrrrrrrrrr	rrrrrrrrrrrrrrrrr			Whirrrrrrrrrrrrrrrrrrrrrrrrrrrrr			
	Well / In		done you		wheel - go!	chairs,		and
	Where		are	the	Play -	sta -	tions™?	
	Beep	beep	beep	beep	shhhhhhhhhhhhhhhhhhhhhhhhh			
	Well / In		done you		Play - go!	sta -	tions™,		and

Our group's object to go into the space shuttle:

1	+	2	+	3	+	4	+
Where		are	the	_____?			
Well		done		_____,		and	
In		you		go!			

Music Express Year 3 © A & C Black 2002
www.acblack.com/musicexpress

THE HAPPIEST TIME OF YEAR

1 **Sing the song** *The happiest time of year*

- Teach the song *The happiest time of year.*

> Ding ding-a-ding-a-ding-a-dong,
> The bells are ringing loud and clear.
> Ding ding-a-ding-a-ding-a-dong,
> This is the happiest time of year.

> Merry Christmas, Merry Christmas, one and all,
> Joy to each and ev'ry creature, great and small, singing:

> Ding ding-a-ding-a-ding-a-dong,
> The bells are ringing loud and clear.
> Ding ding-a-ding-a-ding-a-dong,

> This is the happy time of year.
> Ding ding-a-ding-a-ding-a-dong! Yeah!

Teaching tips

- Practise the words of the song very slowly, especially:
  ding ding-a-ding-a-ding-a-dong.
- Can you hear the beginnings of all the words, eg the 'd' of 'ding'?
- Discuss the structure of the song with the class. It has three sections: chorus, verse, chorus, but they will notice that the second chorus ends differently for a more spectacular ending.

- All sing the song through several times to become really familiar with it, then add a steady beat using untuned percussion instruments.

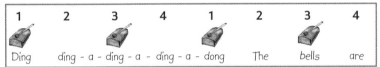

1	2	3	4	1	2	3	4
Ding	ding - a - ding - a - ding - a - dong			The		bells	are

Teaching tips

When listening to your recording, think about:

- whether the singing can be heard above the instruments;
- whether you can hear the beginnings of all the words, especially the 'd' on 'ding';
- whether the ostinato patterns all sound in time - is everyone following the same beat;
- whether the singing was expressive, eg the verse might be sung more quietly than the two choruses.

2 **Practise rhythm patterns from the song as accompaniments**

- Explain that a rhythm pattern repeated throughout a section of music is called an ostinato.

- Using a selection of untuned percussion instruments, invite a group to play an ostinato throughout the song to the rhythm of the words, 'Ding ding-a-ding' *(track 25):*

1	2	+	3	4	1	2	+	3	4
Ding	ding	-	a - ding,			Ding	ding	- a - ding, ...	

- Invite another group to play an ostinato during the verse and second chorus to the rhythm of the words, 'Merry Christmas' *(track 26):*

1	2	3	4	1	2	3	4
Mer	- ry	Christ	- mas,	Mer	- ry	Christ	- mas, ...

3 **Perform** *The happiest time of year* **with a steady beat and two rhythm ostinati**

- Practise performing the song in four groups:
  - one group sings;
  - another group plays the steady beat;
  - two groups perform the ostinati practised in activity 2.

- Record a performance. *(If you decide to perform without the CD, play four beats on the starting note, C', to begin.)*

- Listen to the recording and appraise it as a class.

CHRISTMAS CATS

1 **Listen to a rhythmic rendition of the poem** *Cats*

- Listen to *Cats (track 27)* and discuss where cats like to sleep. *(All the places indicated in the poem. You might like to listen to the poem a few times to hear all the different places mentioned.)*

- Listen to the poem again, all tapping their knees in time with the steady beat:

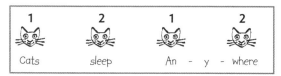

1	**2**	**1**	**2**
Cats	sleep	An - y - where	

- Notice how the syllables of the words make rhythm patterns around the steady beat, eg *(track 28)*:

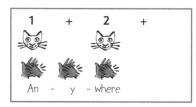 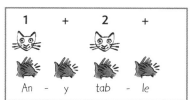

2 **Invent rhythmic new lines for the poem**

- In pairs, think of two new lines for the poem. They should be places a cat might sleep at Christmas time, eg *(track 29)*:

>   Cats sleep
>   Anywhere
>   ✎ Under the mistletoe
>   In the warm
> or
>   ✎ By the presents
>   Under the tree

- Each pair practises saying their lines rhythmically.

3 **Perform** *Christmas Cats*

- Decide an order for each pair to perform their two Christmas lines. Perform *Christmas Cats* as a class, as shown below, tapping a steady beat throughout using fingertips on knees.

All:	Cats sleep Anywhere
Pair 1:	Under the mistletoe In the warm
All:	Cats sleep Anywhere
Pair 2:	By the presents, Under the tree
All:	Cats sleep, Anywhere ...

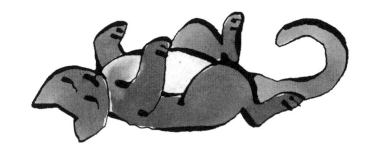

INSTRUMENTAL CHRISTMAS CATS

1 **Play *Christmas Cats* on tuned and untuned percussion**

- In the same pairs as in the last lesson, each pair practises playing the rhythm of their two lines of the *Christmas Cats* poem on untuned percussion instruments, eg

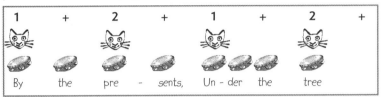

1	+	2	+	1	+	2	+
By	the	pre	- sents,	Un -	der	the	tree

Teaching tips
- The children should imagine the words in their head as they play their instrument, to keep the pattern rhythmic.
- The children may like to take it in turns playing the melody of the first two lines.

- Each pair should practise keeping in time together and repeating their rhythm pattern over and over as an ostinato.

- Practise singing the first two lines of the poem with the CD *(track 30)*. Invite a pair to play the melody on tuned percussion.

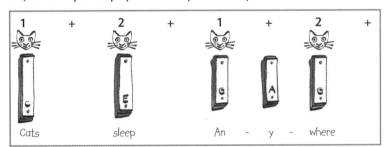

1	+	2	+	1	+	2	+
Cats		sleep		An -	y -	where	

- Practise *Christmas cats* with the CD. All sing the melody of the first two lines, then each pair in turn plays the rhythm of their two lines on untuned percussion instruments.

2 **Practise playing *Christmas Cats* with instrumental ostinati**

- Practise *Christmas Cats* in the following way for a class performance.

  - Establish the steady beat on jingle bells and high and low C chime bars for four beats.

  - A pair plays the melody of the opening two lines of the poem on tuned percussion in time with the steady beat, and everyone else sings.

  - Each pair takes it in turns to play the rhythm of their two lines. They continue repeating the rhythm over and over as an ostinato in time to the beat while other pairs join in.

  - Once every pair is playing their rhythm at the same time, concentrate on all keeping in time to the beat.

  - Decide in advance how to end the piece, eg at a given signal end the piece with a loud declaration 'Cats Sleep Anywhere!'

3 **Perform the instrumental version of *Christmas Cats***

- Record a performance of *Christmas Cats.*

- Listen to your recording and discuss how well the class performed, eg

  - do all the groups keep in time to the same steady beat?

  - does the perfomance start and finish with silence?

Teaching tips
- Encourage everyone to keep singing when they start their ostinato.
- Check everyone knows the class order.

WHAT'S AN ACCOMPANIMENT?

1 Discuss what we mean by accompaniment in music

- Ask the children what they understand by the musical word 'accompaniment'.
  (*An accompaniment may be played on instruments or sung. It might be one or more instruments or voices. It supports the main part - the part which is often playing or singing the melody.*)

- Which instruments have they heard accompanying songs?
  (*Piano and guitar are very common.*)

- Listen to *How doth the little crocodile* (track 31). Ask the children which instruments accompany this song.
  (*It is accompanied by voice and finger clicks.*)

Background information

- The piano accordion is said to have been invented in Vienna in 1829.

- It is a box-shaped instrument which comes in different sizes (*the illustration shows a medium-sized one*). On one side is a piano keyboard, and on the other side are buttons which play chords when pressed.

- The sound is made by squeezing the bellows using the arm on the buttons side. Inside there are metal reeds which vibrate as the air squeezes through them.

2 Listen to different ways in which instruments accompany a song

- Listen to a selection of songs. Ask the children to identify the accompanying instrument.

  – *Flyblown blues* (track 32) is accompanied by a piano.

    Why do they think this is an effective accompaniment?
    (*The piano is playing in a way that compliments the blues style of the song and the humour of it.*)

  – *Dumplins* (track 33) is accompanied by a guitar.

    Listen to the same song accompanied by the piano (track 34). Which recording do the children prefer?

  – *Clap your hands* (track 35) is accompanied by a piano accordion.

    Explain what a piano accordion is if the children have never heard of it before.

- Listen to a selection of songs accompanied by more than one instrument. Ask the children which instruments are playing.

  – An extract from *Ein Mädchen oder Weibchen* from Mozart's opera *The magic flute* (track 36) is accompanied by a whole orchestra.

  – *Sea slugs and jellyfish* (track 4) and *Battle song of the Zartians* (track 37) are accompanied by electronic sounds.

3 Sing the accompaniment to *How doth the little crocodile*

- All practise singing the vocal accompaniment to *How doth the little crocodile* with finger clicks along with the CD.

- Invite individuals to play the finger click pattern on untuned percussion.

- Practise singing and playing in time with the CD.

HILL AN GULLY

1 Work with the melody of *Hill an gully*

- Listen to *Hill an gully* (track 38). Explain that this is a call and response song - the call may differ, but the response is always the same.

Call:	Response:
Hill an gully rida,	Hill an gully.
Hill an gully rida,	Hill an gully.
An ah ben dung low dung,	Hill an gully.
An a low dung bessy dung,	Hill an gully.

- All sing the song with the CD.

- Sing the song again and invite individuals to join in playing the rhythm of the response on tuned percussion on the note D - see the *Call and response* photocopiable.

Background information

- *Hill an gully* is a traditional Jamaican work song which used to be sung by workers constructing new roads.
- The words of the song refer to the uneven and hazardous terrain through which the new road had to be cut.
- *bessy dung* - bend down

Teaching tips

- To work something out by ear, listen carefully to the spaces between the notes:
  - is the next note higher, lower or the same?
  - is there a big gap or are the notes next door to each other?
- Encourage the children to sing the melody quietly to help them work it out. You might like to play the CD track several times.
- Members of the class might like to use their own instruments to work it out.

2 Identify and play by ear a melodic phrase of *Hill an gully*

- In groups, or as a whole class, work out the melody of the first line of *Hill an gully* by ear. Tell the class that the melody starts on the note A, and uses some, but not all, of the following tuned percussion notes: D E F# A B and C'. The shape of the melody is given on the photocopiable.

- When they have worked out the melody together, they fill in the names of the notes on the *Call and response* photocopiable.

Answer (A A A B A F#):

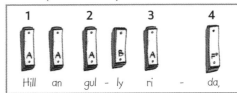

- Divide the class in half. One half plays and sings the calls and the other half the response. Then swap over. *(Those playing the calls will only be able to play the first two calls.)*

3 Explore phrases from *Hill an gully* as an introduction to the song

- Ask the class why songs have introductions.
  (An introduction sets the speed and mood. It is useful when there are many singers, because it gives a cue for them all to start singing at the same time. It sometimes sets up the starting note.)

- Listen to the introduction of *Hill an gully*. Ask how useful it is.
  (It sets the speed and gives the starting note, but without giving the performers much time to be ready.)

- As a class, invent an introduction for *Hill an gully* that sets the speed and gives the starting note. They might include phrases from the song, eg

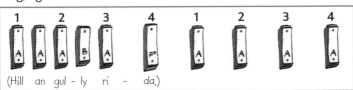

Teaching tips

- A phrase is a short unit of music that often corresponds to a line of a song.
- In *Hill an gully*, 'phrase' can describe the short melodies of the call and of the response.

- Try the children's ideas without the CD. Play the introduction at a chosen speed, then all sing. Could everyone find the speed and starting note? Try different speeds.

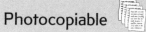
Call and response

Work out the melody of the Call using these notes:

| I | 2 | 3 | 4 | I | 2 | 3 | 4 |

Call: **Response:**

Hill   an   gul - ly   ri   -   da,   Hill   an   gul - ly.

Hill   an   gul - ly   ri   -   da,   Hill   an   gul - ly.

An ah ben   dung   low   dung,   Hill   an   gul - ly.

An ah low   dung   bes - sy dung,   Hill   an   gul - ly.

OL MAS CHARLIE

1 Explore the different beats of *Ol Mas Charlie* p28

- Listen to **Ol Mas Charlie**.

- Play the track again, all adding either of these steady beats using body percussion (*the Charlie's ostinati photocopiable will help the children to follow the beat*):

- When everyone can confidently keep a steady beat, all join in with the singing. Individuals may like to play their steady beat using untuned percussion instruments.

> Ol Mas Charlie,
> Him got a bulldog
> Ina him back-yahd,
> An when him get mad,
> Chain have fe chain him,
> Chain have fe chain him.

Background information

- *Ol Mas Charlie* is a traditional Jamaican song.

Teaching tips

- Rhythm patterns often match word rhythms in a song.
- A repeated rhythm pattern is called an ostinato.
- Encourage the children to get into the mood of the piece through the rhythms.

2 Learn some repeated rhythm patterns in *Ol Mas Charlie* p28

- All use the **Charlie's ostinati** photocopiable and track 40 to learn to play the rhythm of the words 'Chain have fe chain him' on body or untuned percussion.

- Play the song again (*track 39*), all repeating the rhythm throughout as an ostinato.

- All learn the rhythm of the phrase 'Him got a bulldog' using the photocopiable and track 41. Play the song again (*track 39*), all repeating this rhythm throughout as an ostinato using body or untuned percussion.

3 Combine rhythm patterns from the song p28

- Divide into four groups:
  - groups 1 and 2 play each of the steady beats;
  - group 3 plays the 'Chain have fe chain him' ostinato;
  - group 4 plays the 'Him got a bulldog' ostinato.

- Appoint a conductor and decide appropriate signals for start and stop, and get louder and quieter.

- The conductor starts groups 1 and 2. When they are secure, the conductor signals for group 3 to add their ostinato. When that is settled the conductor signals for group 4 to join in. Encourage the conductor to conduct getting louder and quieter and to bring the music to a close.

- Invite other children to be the conductor, and explore adding in more rhythmic ostinati (*see photocopiable for ideas*).

The class orchestra
Exploring arrangements

 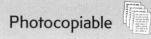
Charlie's ostinati

1	+	2	+	3	+	4	+
Ol		Mas		Char	-	lie	
Him		got	a	bull	-	dog	
In		- a	him	back	-	yahd,	
An		when	he	get		mad,	
Chain		have	fe	chain		him,	
Chain		have	fe	chain		him.	

An ostinato is a pattern that is repeated over and over again.

Ostinato 1

1	2	+	3	4
Chain	have	fe	chain	him, ...

Ostinato 2

1	+	2	+	3	4
	Him	got	a	bull -	dog, ...

Try these as ostinati:

1	2	3	4
Chain			him, ...

1	+	2	+	3	4
Bar -	King	all	day	long, ...	

WHY SING?

1 Identify some of the different purposes of songs

- Ask the children these questions:

  - Where do we hear songs?
    (In school, at celebrations such as weddings, for worship, at a concert, on CDs for enjoyment at home ...)

  - Why do we sing?
    (To entertain others and express how we feel, eg sad, happy ...)

  - What sort of songs do we sing?
    (Some are for enjoyment only, some tell a story, eg an historical event, some are for special purposes, eg a lullaby soothes a baby, others are for special occasions, eg a carol is usually sung at Christmas ...)

- Make a list of some of the songs the class knows and what they are about.

Teaching tip

- Throughout history songs have been inspirational at both a physical and a spiritual level.

2 Listen to a selection of songs which have different purposes

- All join in singing *Hill an gully* (track 38). Consider why work songs were sung.
  (To help those working at repetitive actions, eg building a road, sailors pulling in ropes, working in fields ...)

- What kind of song do the children think *Flyblown blues* is (track 32)?
  (It is a humorous song, it makes us think of an everyday event from a different angle.)

- What kind of song do the children think *Freedom* is (track 42)?
  (It is a song about faith, to inspire worship.)

- Ask the children what the song *Brennan on the moor* is about (track 43).
  (It is an historical song about a highwayman.)

3 Select songs for a radio audience

- Imagine you are preparing a children's hospital radio show. Discuss how you will choose which songs to play. Consider:

  - the different tastes in music of the listeners;

  - the different ages of the patients;

  - the time of day;

  - the different religious beliefs patients may have;

  - the fact that many will have serious illnesses.

- In groups, compile a track list to play, indicating reasons for choosing particular songs.

- Groups share their ideas with the class, then the class agrees a final track list that uses the best suggestions from each group. Keep a record of the final track list and include the reasons for choosing each song.

RADIO JINGLE

1 Create the text for a radio jingle

- Ask the class what a radio jingle is.
  (*A catchy musical verse that both cheers the listener and reminds them which radio station they are listening to.*)

- Invent some suitable words for a children's hospital radio station jingle, eg

  Feeling low?
  Cheer up, tune in
  To the children's hospital radio.

- Make a note of the completed class jingle.

2 Develop the jingle and explore ways of performing the words

- In groups, invent a melody for the jingle. Listen to the three examples on the CD for ideas *(track 44)*.

- Practise different ways of singing the jingle, eg

  - loudly, quietly, whispered

  - fast, slow

  - with as much expression as possible

- Each group sings their jingle melody to the rest of the class.

- As a class, choose a favourite way of singing the jingle. Consider which would be most appropriate for a children's hospital radio show.

- The group that invented the melody for the chosen version of the jingle teaches it to the rest of the class.

Teaching tips

- Encourage the children to experiment freely.

- Some groups may prefer to explore ways of chanting or rapping their jingle.

- Invite groups to demonstrate their work in progress as inspiration for other groups.

3 Finalise the jingle

- Each group invents their own percussion accompaniment for the class jingle.
  (*Some groups use untuned percussion instruments. Others may like to experiment with tuned instruments to see if they can find two notes that would combine with the melody as an effective accompaniment.*)

- Record each group's performance.

- Listen to the recordings and discuss how effective each performance is. Pay particular attention to:

  - how expressively the children sing and play;

  - how well the accompaniment fits with the words;

  - whether the words can be heard clearly;

  - how well they perform together as a group.

CLASS RADIO SHOW

1 Decide upon the structure of the radio show

- As a class, decide who will host the show - this might be the teacher, an individual, or perhaps two children sharing the task.

- As a class, appoint a producer - someone to give cues to members of the class to keep the show running smoothly.

- In advance, arrange for children to bring in CDs of the tracks you will play *(from lesson 4, activity 3)*.

- Discuss a suitable structure and running order for the class show, eg

  – jingle 1

  – host introduction

  – CD track 1

  – jingle 2 and news flash

  – CD track 2

  – jingle 3 ...

- Plan where each group will sit to perform their jingle, and give them time to have a practice.

- Allow time for the host to write a short script, and for small groups to prepare news flashes, if you decide you would like to include some.

- Appoint someone in charge of playing the CDs.

Teaching tips

- Use music you have at school or that the class have borrowed from home.

- Invent some characters to dedicate the music to, this will create a script for the host.

Teaching tips

- Encourage those with speaking roles to take on the confidence of a radio broadcaster.

- Point out that they are communicating something really worthwhile.

- Encourage the class to enjoy their performance.

2 Rehearse then perform the class radio show

- Rehearse the class radio show.
  (You don't need to listen to the tracks all the way through, but it is important to practise all the links so that the show is as seamless as possible. Remind the class that when the show is recorded they can only communicate in silence so it is important that they are all aware of what they are doing and who to watch for cues.)

- When you are prepared, record your work.

3 Listen to and evaluate the recording of the class radio show

- Listen to the recording and evaluate it. Consider which parts worked well and which would need improving, eg

  – was everybody aware of what everyone else was doing?

  – did the show flow smoothly from one section to another, or were there periods of noticeable silence?

  – did those with speaking roles take on their roles convincingly?

  – which jingles were performed well?

  – was the radio show suitable for a children's hospital radio broadcast?

OLD MACDONALD HAD A GLOCK

1 **Sing the song *Old MacDonald had a glock***))

- Teach *Old MacDonald had a glock* (track 45).

  Old MacDonald had a glock, E E D D C.
  And on that glock he had some Cs, E E D D C.
  With a C C here, and a C C there,
  Here a C, there a C, ev'rywhere a C C,
  Old MacDonald had a glock, E E D D C.

- Invite individuals to join in playing the E E D D C on a glockenspiel at the end of the lines. They may also use keyboards or chime bars.

> **Background information**
> - The word 'glock' is short for glockenspiel.
> - A glockenspiel has metal bars.

> **Teaching tips**
> - Demonstrate the shape of the melody with your hands - when the tune goes up, take your hand up in the air, and when the tune comes down, move your hand down.
> - To work out the notes of the melody, listen carefully to the spaces between the notes, eg
>   - is there a big gap or are the notes next door to each other?
>   - is the next note higher, lower or the same as the note you are on?
> - This activity can be done as a whole class or in small groups.

2 **Work out the melody of *Old MacDonald had a glock* by ear**

- Tell the class that the tune starts on the note C. Ask whether the next note *(Mac-)* is the same, higher or lower. *(The same.)* Check this by playing the two notes on tuned percussion.

- All cut out a C chime bar from the **Which pitch?** photocopiable and stick it onto the **Pitch puzzle page 1** above *Mac-*.

- Ask whether the next note *(Don-)* is the same, higher or lower. *(The same.)* Check the answer on tuned percussion and then all cut out another C chime bar and stick it above *Don-*.

- Do the same for each note of the melody. (Photocopiable pages 1 and 2.)
  (NB The first and last lines are exactly the same, as are the first and last notes. Completed photocopiables are provided on the CD- ROM.)

- When the melody is complete, invite several children to perform it while the rest of the class sing.

3 **Identify what is meant by pentatonic scale, using *Old MacDonald had a glock* as an example**

- Ask the children how many different notes are used in this song. *(There are five different notes.)*

- Ask what they are. *(G A C D E)*

- Explain that these five notes are called the C pentatonic scale. It is called pentatonic because there are five notes: the Greek word 'pent' means five. Ask the children to think of other words that have 'pent' in them, eg pentagon and pentathlon.

- Explain that the word 'scale' is taken from the Latin 'scala' meaning a ladder. In a song the notes of a scale are used in any order.

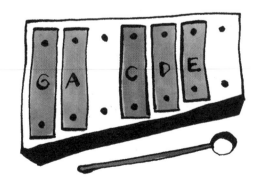

Pitch puzzle page 1

1	2	3	4	1	2	3	4
Old	Mac -	Don -	ald	had	a	glock,	
E	E	D	D	C.			And
on	that	glock	he	had	some	Cs,	
E	E	D	D	C.			With a

Music Express Year 3 © A & C Black 2002
www.acblack.com/musicexpress

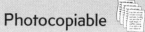
Pitch puzzle page 2

1	2	3	4	1	2	3	4
C	C	here,	and a	C	C	there,	
Here a	C,	there a	C,	ev - 'ry - where a		C,	C,
Old	Mac -	Don -	ald	had	a	glock,	
E	E	D	D	C.			

Which pitch?

Cut out the chime bars you need for the melody.

WHAT YOU GOT?

1 Sing the pentatonic song *What you got?*

- Teach *What you got?* (track 46).

> What you got cooking in the pot?
> Is it sweet and sour, or spicy and hot?
> Is it crunchy? Is it chewy?
> Is it runny? Is it gooey?
> Oh what?
> I can't believe it,
> You've eaten the lot!

> ### Teaching tips
> - Concentrate on learning the words.
> - There are lots of 'te' sounds that need good strong tongue work: what, got, pot, it, hot, don't, eaten, lot.
> - Write out the words of the song, then all try singing it sounding only the words with the 'te' sound. Hear the other words in your head without singing them out loud.

- Explain that the melody of the song only uses the five notes C D E G A, which are the notes of the C pentatonic scale:

2 Accompany the song using notes from the C pentatonic

- Tap a steady beat in time to the song. Invite individuals to play the steady beat on the note E, eg

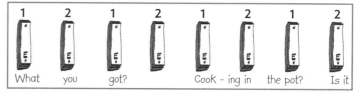

- Play the song again, and invite other children to play the steady beat on other notes from the C pentatonic scale or untuned percussion.

> ### Teaching tips
> - Don't let the accompaniment parts be too loud. When the voices join in, the accompaniment must balance with the volume of sound the voices make.
> - Any of the five notes C D E G A may be used to accompany the song.
> - The children performing the drone should let the sound ring as long as possible when they strike the notes.

- Play the song a third time, and invite individuals to add a drone on the notes C and G as shown below:

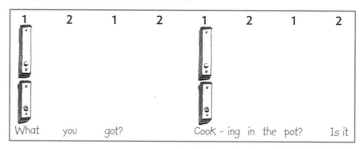

3 Perform and appraise a performance of the song accompanied by notes of the C pentatonic

- Perform *What you got?* to a backing track (track 47) with the tuned and untuned percussion accompaniments practised in activity 2. Invite a small group to be an audience and give feedback on:
  - how clearly the words were sung;
  - how expressive the singing was;
  - the balance of voices to accompaniment.
- Perform the song several times to allow different groups to appraise.

> ### Teaching tip
> - You will hear four beats on the starting note to signal when to begin singing.

PENTATONIC IMPROVISATIONS

1 **Improvise one line of a tune using notes from the C pentatonic scale**

48-49)) p38

- Teach the song *Which notes are these?* using track 48.

  Which notes are these?
  ? ? ? ?
  Which notes are these?
  Can you tell me which they are?

- Invite a volunteer to select one of the performance cards *(photocopiable)*. All sing the song. The volunteer plays the four notes on tuned percussion in the gap after the first line *(listen to the example on track 49)*:

  Which notes are these?

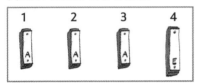

  Which notes are these?
  Can you tell me which they are?

- The class use their hands to show the relative pitch of the notes, eg

  high   same   same   lower

Teaching tips

- Prepare the four performance cards in advance using the photocopiable.
- You may need to sing the song a second time for each player to give the class another chance to remember the pitch.

2 **Improvise a line with a more complex rhythm pattern**

50-51))

- Teach the song *What pattern's this?* using track 50.

  What pattern's this?
  ? ? ? ?
  What pattern's this?
  ? ? ? ?

- Sing the song. Invite volunteers to invent a rhythm pattern that lasts four beats to perform in lines two and four, using body percussion, eg *(track 51)*:

  What pattern's this?

  What pattern's this?

- Sing the song through several times without stopping. Members of the class take it in turns to improvise in lines two and four.

3 **Combine rhythm and melody in *What pattern's this?***

52))

- Sing the song again. This time individuals take it in turns to improvise a melody for lines two and four using any notes of the C pentatonic (C D E G A) in any rhythm pattern, eg *(track 52)*:

  What pattern's this?

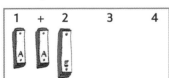

  What pattern's this?

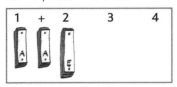

Teaching tips

- Try to ensure that everyone keeps in time with a steady beat.
- Each time you practise, keep the activity flowing – even if a child's pattern goes wrong.
- The more you practise the activity, the easier the children will find it.

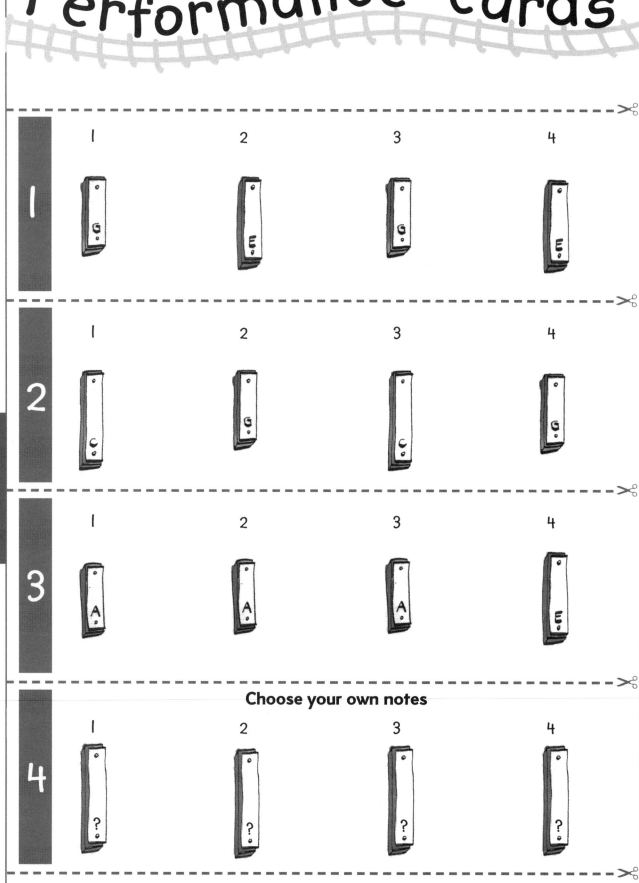

DOUBLE PENTATONIC

1 Sing two pentatonic songs at the same time

- Revise *Old MacDonald had a glock* and *What you got?* (tracks 45 and 46). As you sing each song, all tap a steady beat.

- Listen to a performance of the two songs sung together (track 53). Ask the children why they think the two songs can be sung at the same time.
  (They follow the same steady beat, and only use the notes of the C pentatonic scale.)

- Divide the class into two groups. Practise singing the two songs together with track 53 in the following way, all tapping a steady beat throughout:
  - group 1 sings *What you got?* once through. When they reach the end, they go straight back to the beginning and sing it another two times;
  - group 2 joins in singing *Old MacDonald had a glock* when group 1 starts their song for the second time.

  Explain that the starting notes for each song are played for them on the CD four beats before they start singing.
  *(The starting note for **What you got?** is E and is played on a xylophone. The starting note for **Old MacDonald had a glock** is C and is played on the piano.)*

- When the class is confident, try performing without the CD. Give group 1 four beats on their starting note E to begin. The last line of *What you got?* finishes on the note C which is the starting note of *Old MacDonald had a glock*.

> **Teaching tip**
> - It is a special feature of pentatonic scales that all the notes sound well if played together. This is not true of all scales.

2 Add an accompaniment to *What you got?* and *Old MacDonald had a glock*

- Invite a group to play C G C G throughout on the steady beat using any tuned instruments. Ask the rest of the class to help them keep a steady beat by clapping it quietly while the group practise.

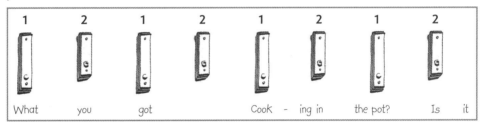

- Ask the class to suggest rhythm patterns that could be played throughout, eg

- Choose an appropriate suggestion and invite another group to play it. Ask the rest of the class to quietly clap the steady beat while they practise.

3 Record and appraise a class performance of the two songs

- Practise singing the two songs together, as in activity 1, with the accompaniment practised in activity 2.

- When the class feels confident, record a performance. Listen back, and ask the class to appraise their performance.

- If you have time, make a second recording with different children playing the accompaniment parts.

> **Teaching tips**
> - Were the words clear?
> - Did their singing bring out the meaning of key phrases, eg 'is it crunchy is it gooey' and 'Oh what, I can't believe it'?
> - Could the singers be heard above the accompaniment?
> - Did everyone keep in time to the same beat?

Dragon scales
Exploring pentatonic scales

DRAGON TALK

1 Learn about the perceptions of dragons in different cultures

- Ask the children what they know about dragons.
- Discuss the contrasting perceptions of dragons in different parts of the world.
- Watch a traditional *Chinese dragon dance* (videoclip 12). Notice in particular the up and down waves of movement.
- Brainstorm some of the characteristics of the Chinese dragon and make a list of associated words (*eg celebrations, new year, on the move, exciting, greedy ...*).

Background information

The dragon is the most used emblem in the art of the Far East, and the most ancient.

In Chinese mythology it is the supreme spiritual power. It represents fertility, wisdom and strength.

In the parades to celebrate Chinese New Year, its function is to drive away evil spirits. During the parade the dragon dancers weave through the streets and try to catch the cabbages or Chinese leaves which are hung from upstairs windows.

In the West and in Christian art, by contrast, the dragon is often a symbol of threat and destruction, hence St George slaying the dragon.

2 Create text for a *Chinese dragon song*

- Watch the videoclip again, then use the list of words compiled in activity 1 to invent short lines of text about the Chinese dragon, eg

  Reaches high, swoops low.

  Gold, red, shimmer, shimmer, shimmer.

- As a class, decide the eight best lines of text that have been invented, and arrange them in a suitable order to form the lyrics of a *Chinese dragon song.*

3 Create music for the *Chinese dragon song*

- Listen to track 54. All perform the following body percussion rhythm throughout in time to the beat:

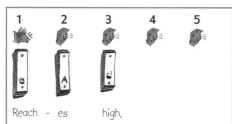

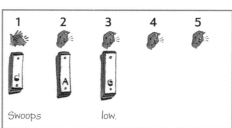

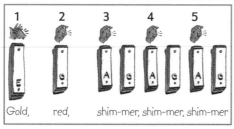

- Divide the class into eight groups, and allocate each group one of the lines of the *Chinese dragon song* from activity 2.
- Using the notes of the C pentatonic scale (C D E G A), each group invents a melody for their line of text, making sure that their melody fits a five-beat pattern. Listen again to the examples on the CD. Notice how the melody reflects the words, eg moves upwards as the dragon reaches high. (*Some groups may want to revise their text to make it fit five beats.*)
- Each group practises singing and playing their melody, then shares their ideas with the class.

Teaching tip
- You will need eight sets of the C pentatonic (C D E G A) - a set for each group.

CHINESE DRAGON SONG

1 **Perform the *Chinese dragon song* to a backing track**

- All listen to the backing track *(track 55)*. Notice that it repeats a steady five-beat accompaniment using notes from the C pentatonic.

- In the same groups as last week, each group practises singing and playing their melodic phrase in time with the five steady beats.

- Once they are confident keeping to the beat of the backing track, rehearse one group after the next, each starting on the first of the five-beat pattern. Rehearse this activity until each group can follow on from the next in time.

Teaching tips
- The backing track repeats the five beat pattern many times.
- Start with an introduction of two sets of the five beats before the first group plays their melodic phrase.
- When all the groups have played their phrase, fade out the CD backing track.

2 **Play the conductor game to perform the *Chinese dragon song***

Teaching tip
- It is helpful if you play the conductor game to the backing track (track 55) in order to keep a steady beat.

- Choose a conductor and devise signals for them to use for start, stop, get louder and get quieter.

- Play the conductor game. With each of the eight groups sitting together, the conductor builds the class piece by selecting the order in which the individual groups perform. Each group sings and plays their phrase over and over when signalled to start by the conductor, and until signalled to stop.

- Take it in turns to be the conductor. As the class becomes more confident with this activity, encourage the conductors to start groups on any beat, not just the first of the five-beat pattern, so that the melodic phrases overlap each other.

3 **Present the class *Chinese dragon song* to a friendly audience**

- Invite an individual to conduct the class performance. As a class, discuss what will make this a sparkling performance, eg
  - all watching the conductor carefully
  - all concentrating
  - starting from silence and finishing with silence
  - all sitting silently when not playing or singing
  - smiling and enjoying the music

- Practise the class *Chinese dragon song.* If you choose to perform without the backing track, you might like to invite a volunteer to play the steady beat throughout on untuned percussion.

- Perform the song to a friendly audience.

Painting with sound
Exploring sound colours

PICTURE THIS

1 Listen to three contrasting pieces of music

- Listen to each track without telling the class the title. What do they think each piece is about, what picture does it create in their mind?

    – *The little train of the Caipira* (track 56)

    – *Ansam* extract (track 57)

    – *Mu min xin ge* extract (track 58)

Background information

- *Ansam* is Arabian. It describes breezes and was composed by Hassan Erraji. It is played on the nay, an Arabian flute.

- *Mu min xin ge* is an instrumental version of a traditional Chinese song. This extract describes a Mongolian cattleman galloping on his horse to round up cattle.

- *The little train of the Caipira* was composed by Villa-Lobos (1897-1959). The music describes travelling through the Brazilian mountains on a steam train.

Nay

2 Discuss the images described in two of the pieces of music

- Explain that each piece listened to in activity 1 was composed to paint a picture in our minds. Music that paints a picture, creates a mood or tells a story is called 'Programme music'.

- Tell the children the image behind *Ansam* (track 57) and *Mu min xin ge* (track 58). Play the extracts again so that the children can hear them in context this time.

- Discuss how each image has been created in the music. There are some ideas below to help:

Ansam

- timbre *(quality of sound)*: the melody is played on a wind instrument and the player makes a breathy sound like the wind.

- rhythm: the melody, like the wind, has no steady beat or regular rhythm. The melody comes and goes - there are gaps where the wind stops then starts again.

- dynamics *(how loud)*: the nay generally plays quietly throughout, although occasionally gets louder which makes us feel the wind gets stronger.

Mu min xin ge

- tempo *(speed)*: we know the horses are galloping rather than walking because of the fast speed.

- rhythm: the accompaniment repeats a rhythm pattern to represent the galloping hooves.

- structure: we can imagine the horses galloping round and round a field because the flute melody is repeated several times.

3 Identify how the image has been created in *The little train of the Caipira*

- Listen again to *The little train of the Caipira* (track 56), having made the title known. What do the children notice about the speed of the train at the beginning? in the middle? at the end?
(It starts slowly, gradually increases speed, makes an emergency stop in the middle, and slows down at the end.)

- Individually or in pairs, the children fill in *The little train* photocopiable. They note down the sound effects they hear in each section of the piece. If they can, encourage them to suggest which instrument makes each sound effect, eg

    – flutes and trombones blare like the train whistle

    – a piano plays fast rhythm patterns round and round like the train wheels

    – a metal shaker and tambourine make a sound like the train's pistons

The little train

What train sounds can you hear in each section? What instruments are playing?

Setting off

Steady speed

Braking hard

Steady speed

Slowing down

Music Express Year 3 © A & C Black 2002
www.acblack.com/musicexpress

SPORTS DAY

1 Discuss the picture *Sports day*

- Look at *Sports day* (CD-ROM picture 1). Ask the children how they know it is about a sports day?
  (There are children running to complete a race, a start and finish line, children wearing rosettes and carrying trophies, a teacher blowing her whistle, parents watching ...)

- Ask the children which parts of the picture involve sound. Make a list.
  (The crowds are clapping and cheering, the teacher is blowing a whistle, a child is crying because he has injured himself, there is a man talking through a microphone, there are children running ...)

Teaching tips

- Encourage the children to think of instruments other than the voice to represent vocal sounds.

- It is important that each suggestion is made first by recalling and describing the sound and then by trying it out.

- Let several children have a go at imagining sounds and playing the sounds that others have imagined.

- Some sounds may need more than one instrument.

2 Play some sounds from the picture

- As a class, select five sounds from the list made in activity 1.

- Invite individuals to suggest an instrument to represent each of the five sounds. The children make their suggestions from their memory of sounds different instruments make, rather than by playing the instruments. They should also specify how to play the instrument.
  (eg, for the child crying they might suggest tapping a cymbal with two rubber-headed beaters as fast as possible.)

- For each suggestion, invite another child to make the sound as described on the chosen instrument. Is the first child satisfied with the sound produced? Does it match their idea of the sound in the picture? If not, they should demonstrate their intentions.

- As a class, discuss how effective each suggestion is for representing the sound in the picture. Think in particular about:
  - whether the sound is the right length/too long/too short;
  - whether the instrument is made from the best material (*wood, skin or metal*);
  - how the sound effect could be improved?

- As a class, choose a favourite way to represent each of the five chosen sounds with instruments.

3 Play the invented music from the picture

- Appoint a conductor, and choose individuals to play each of the five sound effects.

- The conductor uses a pointer to move over the picture. When the pointer arrives at any of the five sounds, the conductor pauses for the instrumentalist to perform the sound effect.
  (The conductor may move their pointer in any direction over the picture.)

- Encourage several children to take turns to be the conductor or one of the five instrumentalists.

Teaching tips

- You can use a ruler or long pencil as a pointer.

- Make sure that everyone can see the picture and where the conductor is pointing.

- The conductor could stand in front of the instrumentalists and use agreed signals to tell them when to start and stop instead of pointing to the picture.

- Watch to see if the conductor structures the piece or if the sounds are selected at random.

Painting with sound
Exploring sound colours
3rd

SUNSET OVER THE SEA

1 **Discuss the picture *Sunset over the sea***

- Look at *Sunset over the sea* (CD-ROM picture 2). Ask the children how many different layers they can see in the picture.
  (There are three main layers: the sand, the sea and the sunset. The children may have different ideas, which is fine, for example they might consider the palm tree as part of the sand layer or a separate layer to the sand.)

- What do the children think the mood of the picture is?
  (Gentle, calm, relaxed, inspiring ...)

- The children imagine they are going to invent some music to be played whilst this picture hangs in a gallery and people look at it. Invite individuals to suggest ways to create the mood of the picture with music.
  (eg the music might be fairly quiet overall to reflect the calmness of the picture, then it might get louder to represent the vibrant red of the sun. Any movement would be very gentle because the sea looks calm, not rough. There might be a steady beat to represent the gentle lapping of the waves. Instruments would be played gently ...)

Teaching tip
- These ideas are suggestions only, the children will come up with their own imaginative ideas.

2 **Compose layers of music to accompany the picture**

- Allocate each layer of the picture to a different group of children in the class. As a class suggest suitable instruments for each layer of sound, eg

  - sand group: rainmakers; maracas turned slowly; cabassas turned slowly; tambourines shaken very quietly;

  - palm tree group *(optional)*: a guiro scraped very slowly and gently; tambours tapped very carefully with fingertips;

  - sea group: ocean drum; metallophones with soft beaters sliding up and down;

  - sunset group: one gentle hit on a large cymbal, letting the sound ring; a solo recorder playing a long note.

- Each group practises their music in turn whilst the class listens. Encourage the children to suggest improvements. Work as a class to develop each layer.

3 **Combine the layers of music and assess how effectively they capture the mood of the picture**

- Build up a piece layer by layer to create a thickening texture which captures the mood of the picture *Sunset over the sea*:

  sand --
  palm tree --
  sea --
  sunset --

- Ask the children what happens to the volume of the music as more layers of sound are added.
  (It gets louder.)

- As a class, discuss how to end the piece.
  (Each layer of music might drop out one by one in reverse order until the sand group remains.)

- Perform the class composition. Invite individuals to take it in turns to look at the picture whilst the class performs to assess how effectively the music captures the mood of the picture. They should consider:

  - whether the music is too loud or too quiet;

  - whether the layers come in too quickly or take too long;

  - whether the layers blend together or if one layer is more prominent.

HAUNTED HOUSE

1 **Learn the song** *Horror Hotel*

- Listen first, then all join in singing *Horror Hotel.*

> Turn right down Sinister Street
> Then cut through Panicky Park,
> Turn left at Cold Feet Lane,
> Where it's always dim and dark,
> Head then for Horror Hotel
> Arising from the gloom,
> You can be sure that you won't sleep well
> But you'll always get a room, for
> The spooky Duke runs this town's hotel,
> What a laugh, it's an empty shell,
> The roof's long gone and the walls as well,
> And your host's a ghost!

- As a class, make a list of the words and phrases in the song that create the spooky description of the hotel.
  (eg sinister, panicky, cold feet, dim, dark, horror, gloom, spooky, empty shell, ghost ...)

2 **Discuss the picture** *Haunted house* **and create a repertoire of vocal haunted sounds**

- Look at *Haunted house* (CD-ROM picture 3). How do the children think the artist has made the house appear haunted?
  (It is dark and misty and one of the clouds has been made to look like a ghost. There is a bat in the sky and the gates are also bat-shaped. The gate is padlocked and no one has been through it for a long time - there is a spider's web. There are scary animals by the gate - a wolf and a raven - as if they are trying to scare people away ...)

- Invite volunteers to demonstrate ways of using their voices to make the scary sounds of the haunted house, eg

  - a ghostly laugh
  - wind in a hollow passage
  - creaking doors
  - a weeping ghost
  - rattling chains
  - a sudden shock
  - teeth chattering
  - feeling frightened

Teaching tips
Encourage groups to think about when to perform their sound effect.

- Some sound effects could be inserted in the gaps between phrases of the song
- Some of the sound effects might be effective if made continuously throughout, like a drone.

3 **Accompany the song** *Horror Hotel* **using the repertoire of vocal haunted sounds**

- As the class sings *Horror Hotel*, invite a group to choose their favourite haunted house sounds to accompany the song. Encourage the group to listen carefully to the singers and make their sound effects appropriately.

- Repeat the activity with different groups performing the sound effects.

SUPERMARKET SCENE

1 Discuss the sounds that could be part of a picture

pic 4

- Look at the picture of a busy supermarket *(CD-ROM picture 4)*. Ask the children what they can see in the picture.

- Ask the children what they would hear if the picture came to life. Make a class list of words and phrases suggested.
(eg checkout noises, background music, overhead announcements, trolleys rattling, baby crying, people talking, bottles falling ...)

2 Discuss appropriate instruments to represent the sounds in the picture

p48

- Divide the class into groups. Each group chooses two of the sounds from the class list.

- Without using any percussion instruments, each group discusses which instruments might be played to represent their two chosen sounds. Encourage them to use the *Ideas sheet* photocopiable for inspiration.

- Invite each group to share their ideas with the class, and explain why they chose particular instruments. Each group then demonstrates what they had imagined on their chosen instruments. As a class, help each group to assess their choices, eg

  – can they make the sound they want on their chosen instrument?

  – do they like the sound produced?

  – is the sound produced effective for representing their chosen sound?

  – how could the sound be improved? *(eg choose a different instrument, play the same instrument in a different way?)*

Teaching tip

- Many groups will find they change their mind about using an instrument having heard it. They will become more skilled at imagining instrumental sounds through trial and error.

3 Prepare sound bites of the picture

- Each group refines their ideas from activity 2 following the class suggestions, and composes two 'sound bites' to represent each of their chosen sounds from the picture.
(Circulate round each group whilst they work to help them develop their sounds into a structured mini composition.)

- Each group makes a note of their two sound bites, including: which instruments they have chosen, reminders of how they play these instruments and in what order.
(It is useful if each group can make a recording of themselves playing their sound bites to remember them for next lesson. They will be used in a class composition.)

Ideas sheet

How long does the sound last?

Is there a steady beat?

Is there a pattern that is repeated?

Is it a high sound or a low sound?

Is it heard continuously or just now and then?

Is the instrument made out of metal or wood?

Is there a strong rhythmic pattern?

Could a keyboard make the sound we want?

Could we create the effect we need by playing two notes together?

Painting with sound
Exploring sound colours

6ᵗʰ

SUPERMARKET COMPOSITION

1 Revise the sound bites from last lesson

- Each group practises their sound bites using their recording and written notes. They might like to make further improvements.

- Write a list of each group's sound bites on a blackboard or somewhere everyone can see.

- Show the class the picture of the supermarket scene again. Discuss which of the sound bites in the list:

  – would be heard more or less continuously (eg trolley wheels and people talking);

  – would occur at regular intervals (eg people dropping items into a shopping trolley);

  – would occur as a one off or irregularly (eg child crying).

Teaching tips

- More than one sound can be playing at any time.
- Sounds can overlap - one can start before another finishes.
- Sounds that would be heard more or less continuously can be repeated over and over (as an ostinato).
- Some sound bites may be effective played one after another, especially if the events occur one after the other.
- It might be useful if some sound bites are repeated at key places in the piece, to help give the piece structure.
- In a piece of music there can be places where only one sound is happening and others where there is a thick texture.
- Pieces of music can include periods of silence, but the class may not feel this is relevant in this instance.

2 Decide how to combine the sound bites to create a supermarket composition

- As a class, discuss ways of combining the sound bites for a class composition. Invite volunteers to demonstrate their ideas, and decide as a class what is the most effective.

- Practise the class supermarket composition so that everyone is clear about when to play.
  (You might like to appoint a conductor to lead the class, and you might like to write a plan of the piece on the blackboard or somewhere everyone can see.)

Teaching tips

- It might be useful to make a label for each sound bite and place them in front of the relevant group as a reminder to the conductor.
- Encourage the conductor to give a very clear signal for start and stop when asking each sound bite to play.
- With more practice the conductors might experiment with increasing the loudness of individual sound bites.

3 Record and evaluate the class supermarket composition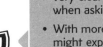

- When the class is confident playing the supermarket composition, make a recording of a performance.

- As a class, listen to the recording whilst looking at the picture and evaluate its success. In particular, think about:

  – whether the composition creates the look and the feel of the picture;

  – what the class would change, if anything.

Salt pepper vinegar mustard
Exploring singing games

SINGING GAMES I

1 Watch and discuss some playground singing games

- Invite volunteers to demonstrate any singing games they know that involve actions, skipping, dancing, counting, choosing someone to be 'it' or ball-work.

- Watch the following singing games on the CD-ROM. Ask the children whether they know any of them:

  - *One potato, two potato (videoclip 13)*

  - *Ip dip (videoclip 14)*

  - *A sailor went to sea, sea, sea (videoclip 15)*

  - *Have you ever (videoclip 16)*

- Ask whether any of these games have a purpose, or are they just for fun?
  (*One potato, two potato* and *Ip dip* are selection games. *A sailor went to sea, sea, sea* and *Have you ever* develop coordination skills.)

2 Try playing each singing game

- As a class, learn the words and melody of each singing game using the CD tracks. Then, when the children are confident singing or chanting the words, all learn the actions using the videoclips and photocopiables.

  - *One potato, two potato (track 60, videoclip 13)*

  - *Ip dip (track 61, videoclip 14)*

  - *A sailor went to sea, sea, sea (track 62, videoclip 15)*

  - *Have you ever (track 63, videoclip 16)*

Teaching tips

- Singing games can be for individuals, pairs or groups of friends.

- Each singing game has a musical feature, an appropriate action and often a particular purpose. As you learn each game make sure the class knows and understands its properties.

3 Explore the musical and physical characteristics of each singing game

- Discuss the actions and musical features in each game (*eg is there a steady beat, are the words chanted or sung, are there different verses, are the same actions used each time, does the game speed up? ...*).

  - *One potato, two potato (track 60, videoclip 13)*
    A repeated chant with a steady beat. Its purpose is to select someone from a group to be 'it'. The same words and action are repeated again and again, gradually eliminating children until someone is selected.

  - *Ip dip (track 61, videoclip 14)*
    A repeated chant made up of nonsense words with a steady beat. Again, the same words and action are repeated until someone has been selected to be 'it'.

  - *A sailor went to sea, sea, sea (track 62, videoclip 15)*
    A game for pairs of players. It has a catchy melody and a steady beat. Different body actions are used for each verse. It can be played getting gradually faster.

  - *Have you ever (track 63, videoclip 16)*
    A game for pairs of players. It has a catchy melody and a steady beat. The actions vary for each verse and children can invent their own. It can be played getting gradually faster.

Selection games

One potato, two potato, three potato, four, five potato, six potato, seven potato more!

Ip dip sky blue, who's it? Not you!

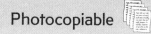
Action games

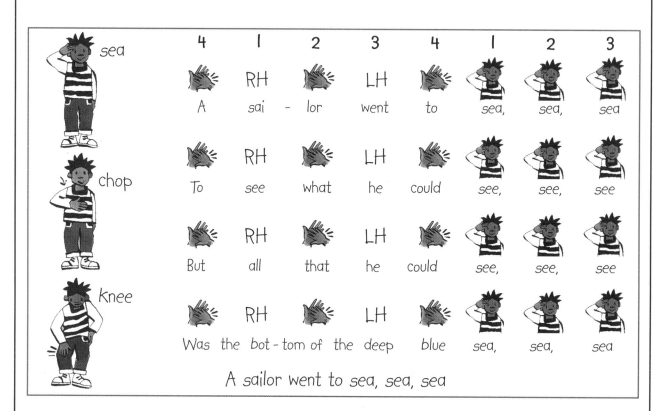

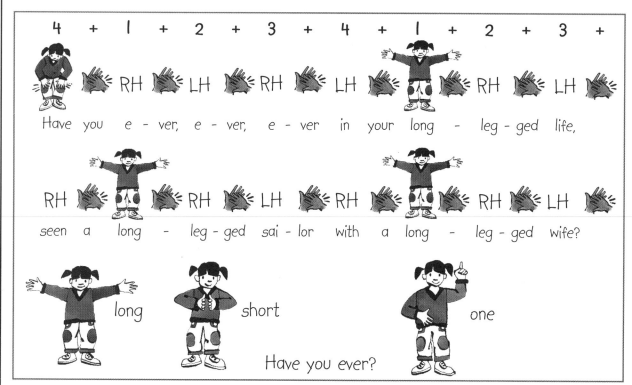

SINGING GAMES II

1 **Perform the singing games from lesson 1 and watch some new games**

- Invite volunteers to demonstrate each of the singing games from lesson 1 *(videoclips 13-16)*.

- As they revise each game, check that the class also remembers its musical features, actions and purpose *(see p50 for details)*.

- Watch four more singing games on the CD-ROM:

    - *High low dolly pepper (videoclip 17)*

    - *Salt pepper vinegar mustard (videoclip 18)*

    - *Over the garden wall (videoclip 19)*

    - *Pass the ball (videoclip 20)*

2 **Try playing four singing games with different actions**

- As a class, learn the words and melody for each singing game using the CD tracks, then learn the games by watching the videoclips and following the photocopiables. As you learn each game, think about the musical characteristics.
(All require a space large enough for bouncing balls and using a skipping rope.)

    - *High low dolly pepper (track 64, videoclip 17)*
    A group skipping game chanted to a steady beat. There are different actions for each word.

    - *Salt pepper vinegar mustard (track 65, videoclip 18)*
    An individual skipping game chanted to a steady beat that gets gradually faster.

    - *Over the garden wall (track 66, videoclip 19)*
    A ball game for pairs of children. It has a catchy melody and a steady beat to which the ball is bounced. A new phrase is added to each verse so that the song gets gradually longer.

    - *Pass the ball (track 67, videoclip 20)*
    A group ball game that has a catchy melody and a steady beat. The same melody is sung each time, but with a different child's name.

3 **Think about the characteristics singing games have in common**

- Explain that singing games are played by children all around the world. *Pass the ball* is from Jamaica.

- Discuss the eight games learnt so far and ask the class to identify any characteristics common to many or all, eg

    - they all have a steady beat and a strong rhythm
    (Salt pepper vinegar mustard got faster, and A sailor went to sea, sea, sea and Have you ever could also get faster.)

    - many have a catchy melody, others were chanted
    (Ip dip, High low dolly pepper and Salt pepper vinegar mustard were chanted, the others had catchy melodies.)

    - they are all very repetitive
    (Some repeated the same chant over and over: Ip dip, High low dolly pepper and Salt pepper vinegar mustard. The others repeated the same verse but with a slight variation each time.)

    - they are all easy to remember and good fun

Background information

- Singing games are often street games or playground games passed on through friends and family.

- They were invented as an immediate source of fun that only required minimum resources.

- They involve any number of people, who must share and work together.

- They are fun enough to motivate us to keep trying, and they help develop co-ordination and musical skills.

- They have a competitive element.

Skipping games

Turn the rope for a friend to skip. All repeat the chant 'high low dolly pepper'. Whichever word they trip on, they then skip in that way:

high
turn the rope raised off the ground so they jump high

low
they skip whilst crouching down low

dolly
they skip in the style of a dolly

pepper
they skip faster

High low dolly pepper

Turn the rope twice on the word mustard.

Start slowly and get gradually faster.

Salt pepper vinegar mustard

Ball games

Over the garden wall

The person in the middle guesses who is holding the ball at the end of the song.

The person holding the ball then gets a turn in the middle.

Pass the ball

Music Express Year 3 © A & C Black 2002
www.acblack.com/musicexpress

PASS THE PEBBLE ON

1 Learn *Pass the pebble on* and move in time to the steady beat 68-69

- All listen to *Pass the pebble on (track 68).*

> Pass the pebble on
> Keep a steady rhythm
> Pass the pebble on
> Keep a steady rhythm
> For you'll be out if you don't keep
> In time to the beat,
> For you'll be out if you don't keep
> In time to the beat.

- In a circle, all listen again and step clockwise round the circle in time to the steady beat counted out on the CD.
- When the children are confident moving in time to the beat, join in with the singing as well.
- Move in time to the steady beat of track 69. This track speeds up and slows down. The aim is that everyone keeps in time, speeding up and slowing down with the beat.

2 Play the game, *Pass the pebble on* 68-69

- All kneel in a circle, each with a beanbag or other item to pass round. As the music plays *(track 68):*
  - on 1, all pick up their beanbag using their right hand;
  - on 2, all put their beanbag down in front of the person on their left;
  - on 1, all move their hand back to pick up another beanbag and deliver it again on 2. And so the game continues;
  - when confident with this, join in with the singing.
- Play the game again, but this time use track 69 which speeds up and slows down. The children will need to listen attentively to follow the beat.

Teaching tips
- In this activity the children explore finding two different pulses.
- Invite several groups of children to try the various percussion accompaniments.

3 Explore two different pulses in *Pass the pebble on* 68

- Arrange the class into an inner and an outer circle.
- Play the game using track 68. The outer group passes their beanbags round in time to the slow, steady beat practised in activity 2. The inner circle passes their beanbags twice as fast. Invite a couple of children from each group to help keep the different beats on untuned percussion instruments.

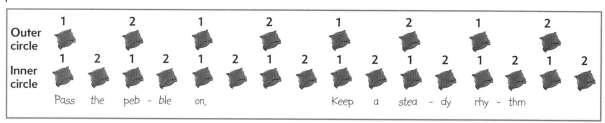

- Try this activity without the CD. Invite volunteers to keep the beat on untuned percussion.

WHAT'S THE GAME?

1 Identify rhythm patterns from different singing games

 p58

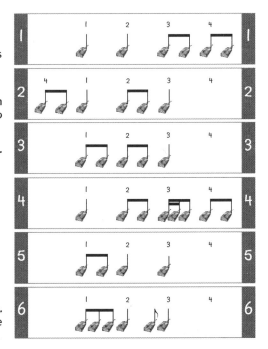

- Enlarge and cut out the six photocopiable cards, which each shows the rhythm of a line from one of the singing games.
(You will need enough sets of the cards for one between two.)

- Show the cards individually to the class and ask whether anyone can recognise where the pattern comes from. *(Encourage the children to try tapping the rhythm on their knees.)*

- Show the cards again as you play a recording of the rhythm pattern. *(You will hear each rhythm played twice.)* Had they guessed right?
  - Card 1 *(track 70)*: High low dolly pepper
  - Card 2 *(track 71)*: In your long legged life
  - Card 3 *(track 72)*: Pass the pebble on
  - Card 4 *(track 73)*: Salt pepper vinegar mustard
  - Card 5 *(track 74)*: Is the ball here
  - Card 6 *(track 75)*: Over the garden wall

- All chant the words for each rhythm pattern along with the CD. Point to each of the wood blocks on the cards as it is played on the CD to give the children the experience of following music notation.

Teaching tips

- The cards are written with conventional musical notation to show children what it looks like and give them the experience of learning it.
- The rhythm patterns can be just as easily accessed through the rhythm of the words of the song.

---

2 Play the rhythm patterns on untuned percussion

- All play the six rhythm patterns on untuned percussion in time with the CD.
(Some children might find it helpful to have a copy of each rhythm card in front of them as they play.)

- Try playing the rhythm patterns without the CD. Give a count in as on the CD, then all repeat each rhythm pattern over and over until everyone is confident playing it.
(Count 1 2 3 4 out loud for everyone to keep in time.)

- Invite pairs to challenge each other to play each of the rhythm patterns at random.

3 Play the game, *Pass the pebble on*, with ostinato accompaniments

  p58

- Shuffle the cards and give one to each person, who places it face down in front of them.

- Play *Pass the pebble on* once through using the cards instead of beanbags.
(Use the CD track or invite a volunteer to keep the steady beat on a drum.)

- All turn over the card they have received. All those with card 1 leave the circle, select an untuned percussion instrument and play the rhythm pattern on their card during the next repetition of the game.

- Play the game again, and all turn over their card at the end, as before. This time those with card 2 leave the circle, select an untuned percussion instrument and play the rhythm pattern on their card during the next repetition of the game. Group 1 also plays their rhythm.

- Continue playing the game, and see how many different rhythmic ostinati you can play at the same time with the song in time to the steady beat.

- For an added challenge, try playing the game faster. Can everyone keep in time?

4th
Salt pepper vinegar mustard
Exploring singing games

Photocopiable

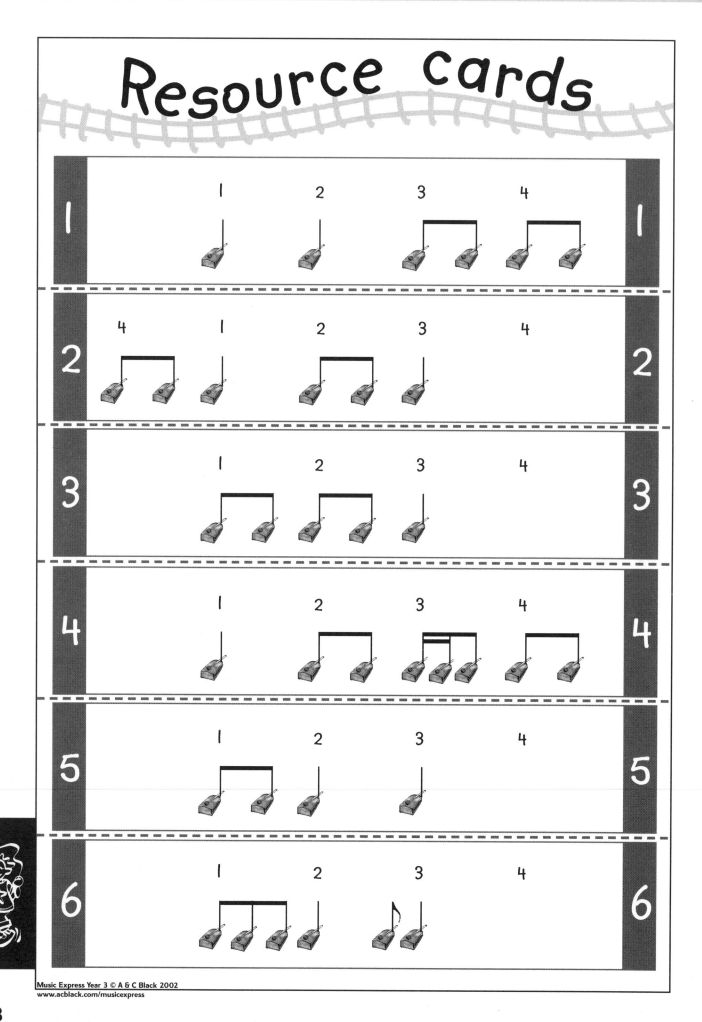

Music Express Year 3 © A & C Black 2002
www.acblack.com/musicexpress

INVENTING SINGING GAMES

1 Create some text for a singing game

- As a whole class, or in groups of at least four, decide whether to create a selection game, an action game, a skipping game or a ball game.

- Create lyrics for the chosen type of singing game, either by adapting the lyrics for the singing game below, or creating some new. *(eg to make this a counting game they might substitute the lines 'Where are you going to, can I come too?' with 'How many are going, can I come too?' and then count rather than give place names.)*

> Skies are blue
> For travelling with you,
> So where are you going to,
> Can I come too?
> Places beginning with C:
> Caribbean,
> Carlisle,
> Canada
> Corner shop etc

Teaching tips
- This is a basic idea, children can be more creative.
- If groups decide to create their own lyrics, remind them that they could be nonsense words or short rhyming poems like the example.

- Try out the lyrics by all chanting them to a steady clapped beat, eg

1	2	1	2
Skies	are	blue for	tra-vell-ing with you, so

2 Listen to and copy melodic phrases on the CD

 p60

Teaching tip
- Some pairs might like to use keyboards or their voices, or bring in instruments from home to play this game.

- All listen to five melodic phrases on the CD *(tracks 76-80)*. After each phrase, the children copy what they hear with their singing voice.

- As a class, work out how to play each of the melodic phrases on tuned percussion, using the *Playing melodies* photocopiable.

- In pairs, play a question and answer game using tuned percussion. The first of the pair asks the question shown on the photocopiable *(track 81)*, and the second child makes up a simple answer. They take it in turns to ask the question and give the answer. What do they think is being asked, and what is the answer?

3 Compose a melody for the singing game

- In the same groups as in activity 1 (or as a whole class), each group composes a melody for the text of their game using tuned percussion instruments. They should write it down for next lesson. Encourage the children to think about:
  - whether the melody leads anywhere *(eg melody 1 (track 76) leads back to the starting note, whereas melody 3 (track 78) seems unfinished)*;
  - whether the melody has a shape *(eg melody 5 (track 80) starts low, gradually gets higher and comes down again)*;
  - whether the melody is simple to sing and easy to remember;
  - what all singing games have in common *(they are repetitive, have a steady beat and a strong rhythm, a catchy melody, and are easy to remember ...)*.

Teaching tips
- G - E is a common interval to sing and is used in many chants.
- The melody they compose need only use a few notes.
- It will be more effective as a playground song if it is simple.
- Suggest they make the melody move by step or small jumps, and put lots of repetition in it.
- Some lines may be played using the same melody.
- Encourage them to hum the melody that they are creating thoughout.

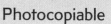
Playing melodies

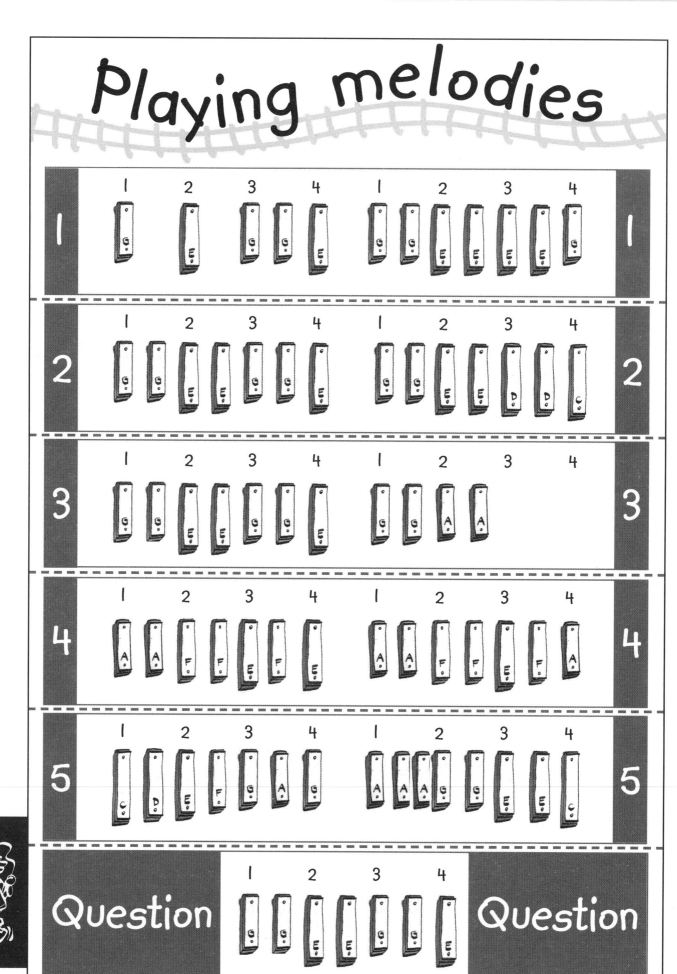

PLAYING SINGING GAMES

1 Complete the singing game with actions

- All revise their singing game song from last lesson.
  (They will need the same tuned percussion instruments they used last lesson.)

- When everyone is happy with the words and melody, they think about the actions that would be suitable for their song. *(If you have been working as a whole class to write the words and melody, now divide into groups to devise the actions.)* In particular, they should think about:

  – where the actions come in the song;

  – how they relate to the speed of the game.

- Encourage each group to write down instructions for remembering the game.

> ### Teaching tip
> - Groups may prefer to chant their singing game rather than sing it. This is fine.

2 Each group presents its game to the class

- Each group performs their game to the class, and records it on video or audio tape.

- Discuss each group's work as a class, giving positive feedback as well as pointers for improvement. Think about:

  – how catchy the melody is;

  – how easy the words are to remember;

  – whether the group performed the game in time with each other;

  – how well the actions fit with the song.

3 Each group teaches another group its game

- Each group learns another group's game to see how fun it is to play.

Index

Index of song titles and first lines

Index of listening tracks

Videoclips

Track   Contents

Track   Contents

NB There are also 17 videoclips for teachers
(see introduction notes p6)

Audio CD track list

Track Contents

Animal magic

1   *Tortoise song* (page 8)
2   Tortoise song verses with counting (8)
3   Tortoise tune - chime bar melody (8, 9)
4   *Sea slugs and jellyfish* (10, 24)
5   *Seagulls* - unsung version (10)
6   *Seagulls* - sung version (10)
7   *Carnival of the animals, Tortoises* (10)
8   *Carnival of the animals, Kangaroos* (10)
9   *Carnival of the animals, The elephant* (10)
10   *Bear dance* (10)
11   *Raga abhogi* -1st part (11)
12   *Raga abhogi* - 2nd part (11)
13   Animal walking (13)
14   Flying/gliding/swooping/swimming (13)
15   Takes off, flies, lands (13)
16   Walks, runs, jumps (13)

Play it again

17   *Polka* (16)
18   Chopsticks pattern (16)
19   *Please, Mr Noah* rap (17)
20   *Please, Mr Noah* rap with gaps (17)
21   Space shuttle rap outline (19)
22   Space shuttle rap example (19)
23   *Space shuttle rap* with gaps (19)
24   *The happiest time of year* (21)
25   'Ding ding-a-ding' ostinato (21)
26   'Happy Christmas' ostinato (21)
27   *Cats* (22)
28   Cats rhythms: 'any table', 'anywhere' (22)
29   Christmas Cats example (22)
30   Christmas cats example + rhythms (23)

The class orchestra

31   *How doth the little crocodile* (24)
32   *Flyblown blues* (24, 29)
33   *Dumplins* - accompanied by guitar (24)
34   *Dumplins* - accompanimed by piano (24)
35   *Clap your hands* (24)
36   *Ein Mädchen oder Weibchen* (24)
37   *Battle song of the Zartians* (24)
38   *Hill an gully* (25, 29)
39   *Ol Mas Charlie* (27)
40   'Chain have fe chain him' ostinato (27)
41   'Him got a bulldog' ostinato (27)

Track Contents

42   *Freedom* (29)
43   *Brennan on the moor* (29)
44   Sample radio jingles (30)

Dragon scales

45   *Old MacDonald had a glock* (32, 39)
46   *What you got?* (36, 39)
47   *What you got? - accompaniment only* (36)
48   *Which notes are these?* (37)
49   Which notes are these? example (37)
50   *What pattern's this?* (37)
51   What pattern's this? rhythm example (37)
52   What pattern's this? melody example (37)
53   *Old MacDonald/What you got?* (39)
54   Dragon music example (40)
55   Dragon song backing track (41)

Painting with sound

56   *Little train of the Caipira* (42)
57   *Ansam extract* (42)
58   *Mu min xin ge extract* (42)
59   *Horror hotel* (46)

Salt pepper vinegar mustard

60   *One potato, two potato* (50)
61   *Ip dip* (50)
62   *A sailor went to sea, sea, sea* (50)
63   *Have you ever* (50)
64   *High low dolly pepper* (53)
65   *Salt pepper vinegar mustard* (53)
66   *Over the garden wall* (53)
67   *Pass the ball* (53)
68   *Pass the pebble on* (56)
69   *Pass the pebble on - changing speed* (56)
70   Rhythm pattern 1 (57)
71   Rhythm pattern 2 (57)
72   Rhythm pattern 3 (57)
73   Rhythm pattern 4 (57)
74   Rhythm pattern 5 (57)
75   Rhythm pattern 6 (57)
76   Melodic phrase 1 (59)
77   Melodic phrase 2 (59)
78   Melodic phrase 3 (59)
79   Melodic phrase 4 (59)
80   Melodic phrase 5 (59)
81   Melodic question (59)

Acknowledgements

The author and publishers would like to thank all the teachers and consultants who assisted in the preparation of this series: Meriel Ascott, Francesca Bedford, Chris Bryant, Yolanda Cattle, Stephen Chadwick, Veronica Clark, Tania Demidova, Adrian Downie, Veronica Hanke, Jocelyn Lucas, Helen MacGregor, Carla Moss, Danny Monte, Lio Moscardini, Sue Nicholls, Vanessa Olney, Mrs S. Pennington, Pauline Quinton, Sheena Roberts, Ana Sanderson, Jane Sebba, Heather Scott, Michelle Simpson, Debbie Townsend and Joy Woodall.

The author and publishers would like to thank Winston Lewis, Debbie Sanders, Missak Takoushian and Vivien Ellis for performing for the recording of this CD. Thanks are also due to all those who performed for previous recordings for A & C Black publications which have been reused in Music Express Year 3.

Special thanks are due to Helen MacGregor, Shaila Thiru and the Year 1 and 3 children of Brunswick Park Primary School for demonstrating and performing for the filming for the CD-ROM videoclips.

The following have kindly granted permission for the reprinting of copyright material in the book:

Ana Sanderson for the words of **What you got?** © 2002 Ana Sanderson, A & C Black Publishers Ltd?

David Higham Associates for **Cats** by Eleanor Farjeon. By permission of David Higham Associates Ltd.

David Sheppard for the words of **Tortoise song** © David Sheppard 2002.

Jeremy Sans for the words of **The happiest time of year**, © 1999.

The following copyright holders have kindly given their permission for the inclusion of their copyright material on the CD:

Ansam Recording © Saydisc Records, England Publishing © Matchbox Music, England

Battle song of the Zartians from BBC Publication Time and Tune Spring 1965, with words by Jenyth Worsley.

Cats by Eleanor Farjeon. By permission of David Higham Associates Ltd.

Ein Mädchen oder Weibchen from Die Zauberflote performed by Drottingholm Concert Theatre directed by Ostman © Polygram. Cat no Decca Classics 440 085 2.

How doth the little crocodile © 1995 Malcolm Abbs.

Kangaroos, The Elephant and **Tortoises** from **Carnival of the Animals** by Saint Saëns. Digitally remastered ℗ 1991 the copyright in this sound recording is owned by EMI Records Ltd. Licensed courtesy of EMI Records Ltd.

Mu Min Xin Ge performed by Li He taken from the album Classical Chinese Folk Music (EUCD 1564) courtesy of ARC Music Productions International Ltd p and © 2002.

Polka by Borodin. Recording CD 66984. Courtesy of Hyperion Records Ltd, London.

Raga abhogi taken from The Raga Guide CD NI 5536, Wyastone Estate Limited, trading as Nimbus Records, www.wyastone.co.uk

The happiest time of year words and music © Jeremy Sans 1999.

The little train of the Caipira by Heitor Villa-Lobos, performed by the London Symphony Orchestra, conducted by Sir Eugene Goossens. An Everest recording, courtesy of the Omega Record Group Inc.

Tortoise song words and music © David Sheppard 2002, A & C Black Publishers Ltd

What you got? words and music © 2002 Ana Sanderson, A & C Black Publishers Ltd

All other recordings are © A & C Black:

Flyblown blues, and **Sea slugs and jellyfish** by David Moses, **Seagulls** by Jane Sebba, **Please, Mr Noah rap** and **Horror hotel** by Kaye Umansky

Bear dance, Clap your hands, Dumplins, Hill an gully, Ol Mas Charlie, Freedom, Brennan on the moor, Old MacDonald had a glock, Which notes are these?, What pattern's this?, A sailor went to sea, sea, sea, Have you ever, High low dolly pepper, Ip dip, Over the garden wall, Pass the ball, Pass the pebble on, and **Salt pepper vinegar mustard** are all traditional songs, arranged and recorded by A & C Black.

Videoclips

Chinese dragon dance courtesy of BSkyB Ltd.

Music Express Year 3 CD and CD-ROM © and ℗ 2002 A & C Black Publishers Ltd. All rights of the owner of the works reproduced reserved. Unauthorised copying, hiring, lending, public performance and broadcasting of these recordings and videoclips prohibited.

Every effort has been made to trace and acknowledge copyright owners. If any right has been omitted, the publishers offer their apologies and will rectify this in subsequent editions following notification.